ALL-AGE EVENTS AND WORSHIP

BOOKS BY THE SAME AUTHOR
AVAILABLE FROM MARSHALL PICKERING

Assembly Praise
Teaching the Bible to Children
Themes for Family Worship

ALL-AGE EVENTS AND WORSHIP

An introduction and guide

Tony Castle

Marshall Pickering
An Imprint of HarperCollinsPublishers

Marshall Pickering is an Imprint of
HarperCollins*Religious*
Part of HarperCollins*Publishers*
77–85 Fulham Palace Road, London W6 8JB

First published in Great Britain
in 1994 by Marshall Pickering

1 3 5 7 9 10 8 6 4 2

A catalogue record for this book is
available from the British Library

ISBN 0 551 02819-X

Printed and bound in Great Britain by
HarperCollinsManufacturing Glasgow

Dedicated to Sarah
– as promised

Acknowledgments

In the preparatory stages of this book I wrote to more than sixty people to research what was happening in all-age worship in the United Kingdom. I am indebted to the following for their helpful replies and suggestions:

The Rev. Mike Sheffield of Ryde, Isle of Wight; the Rev. Brenda Wallace of Stansted, Essex; Canon David Knight of Chelmsford; Mrs Judith Sadler, Diocesan Children's Adviser of the Diocese of Newcastle; the Rev. Peter Jackson of Alwoodley, Leeds; Canon Paul Warren of Standish, Wigan; the Rev. Peter Ingrams of Sheet, Petersfield, Hants; the Rev. Patrick Tuft of Chiswick, London; Canon Ralph Mallinson of Rossendale, Lancs; Canon Michael Sadgrove of Coventry Cathedral; Bishop Colin Buchanan of the Diocese of Rochester; the Rev. Michael Ainsworth of Withington, Manchester; the Rev. Jeremy Haselock of the Diocese of Chichester; the Rev. Gordon Jeannes of St Chad's College, Durham; the Rev. Keith Jones of Ipswich; the Rev. Andrew Nunn of Richmond Hill, Leeds; the Bishop of Peterborough; the Rev. Barry Fenton, Chaplain Precentor of Portsmouth Cathedral; the Rev. John Richardson of Bradford Cathedral; the Rev. G. Clarke of Leicester; the Rev. Francis Minay of Bolton Percy, North Yorkshire; and the Rev. Charles Taylor of Bassett, Southampton.

The author and publishers are grateful to the following for the use of their copyright material:

The Very Rev. Canon C. Walker for the prayer of the Jesus Caritas Fraternity.

The Franciscan Printing Press of Jerusalem for the drawing of Peter's house at Capernaum.

Church House Publishing for an extract from 'The Promise of His Glory'.

Contents

Introduction

Many years ago I was out for a Sunday afternoon walk in the Sussex countryside with some fellow students. We were strolling along a narrow lane, through woods, when we became separated. I stayed on the lane, while a couple of the others were chasing one another through the woods. Beside where I stood was an old wooden five-bar gate, lying at an angle.

As I stood there I became aware of the silence, then of a strange feeling of internal warmth. Then like a bolt out of the blue, with intense clarity I suddenly appreciated something that had escaped me before. It was all at once vividly real and vitally important. 'I live now, not I, Christ lives in me' (in the Bible translation I was then familiar with) means just what it says. Christ dwells by faith in my heart. It suddenly became clear, my prayers must not drift up, like incense, into the presence of God, a God away up and out there somewhere. Personal prayer is to Christ within.

More than thirty years later I can still 'see' the five-bar gate in my mind's eye. That very real experience made a lasting impact upon my approach to my private prayer.

Christianity is not a private religion; it is a community faith. No one can be a private Christian, saying private prayers alone with no membership of and meeting with other Christians; that is a modern heresy. Faith bestows not only a relationship with the Father, but simultaneously a brother/sister relationship with Christ and every other member of the Christian family.

The very first Christian sermon by the Apostle Peter (Acts 2:37–41) makes this clear. After asking how they should respond to Peter's words, the crowd are told, 'Repent and be baptized'. 'Those who accepted his message were baptized, and about three thousand were added to their number that day.' This believing community were faithful to the teaching of the Apostles and worshipped together every day in the temple and met together in one another's homes for the breaking of bread.

One gets the distinct impression that this was a group of believers who were as involved with one another as with God, in worship. So much so that 'all the believers were together and had everything in common' (Acts 2:44).

There are therefore two essential dimensions to every Christian's prayer life: public prayer and private prayer. On countless occasions in the past preachers have attempted to make clear that the cross of Christ points heavenward, symbolic of the adoration of the transcendent God; and the horizontal cross bar, bearing the outstretched arms of Christ, embraces the peoples of the world. This is where the immanent God is to be found.

If Christ dwells by faith in my heart, then he equally dwells by faith in the hearts of each of my brothers and sisters in the Faith. So at the heart of every Christian community is the presence of the Risen Christ, 'for where two or three come together in my name, there am I with them'. All day, and every day, around the world, in and through the innumerable Christian communities, the

Risen Christ is giving adoration and praise to the Father.

All this is in clear contradiction to the injurious individualism of our time. There is the mistaken notion abroad, in all our communities, that church attendance is primarily for the betterment and satisfaction of the individual. The comment 'I did not get anything out of the service, so I stopped going' has a familiar ring to it. The Sunday service, however, is not for collective private prayer, or to give a churchgoer an uplifting experience.

The community of believers, of whatever locality, gathers on the first day of the week to celebrate with the Risen Christ his conquest over death and the powers of darkness, and with Christ the Lord to offer to the Father that adoration and praise which are his due. In a Eucharistic service the individual Christian's union with her/his Lord is all that closer. It binds the community more deeply together and nourishes the spiritual life of the individual and the community.

The primary purpose, then, of Christian public worship is to accord our Creator Father, through the Saviour Son, inspired and led by the Holy Spirit, the praise and thanksgiving that we, his creatures, owe him.

Modern, mobile consumers can shop where they choose. With the light touch of a button they can flash from one TV channel to the next and equally drive to the church of their choice. Should churches be concerned about numbers and cater for people's needs and tastes in public worship? The answer lies in an understanding of the nature of liturgy. It is the people, the whole community, that worship; not the clergy, with the laity present as spectators. What characteristics should mark good public worship, which attracts and involves?

All-Age Worship:

> *'I am the music man*
> *I come from down your way*
> *And I can play...*
> *What can you play?*
> *I can play the bagpipes* (action)
> *I can play the piano* (action)
> *I can play the trombone* (action)

It was eight-thirty in the evening and in a huge heaving mass the people – children and grandparents, teenagers and parents, single people and couples – were joyously jigging up and down, singing along to the disco music. Two hundred or more people throwing themselves wholeheartedly into the action songs. The place? The large ballroom of a holiday centre in August last year, where my family and I were enjoying a summer break.

As I witnessed this all-age fun I remembered the half-finished manuscript of this book lying at home in my study. Before me was a magnificent celebration of the family and a wonderful example of down-to-earth innocent human happiness. The ingredients were lively music, plenty of encouragement to participate, good confident leadership and simple actions for people, of all ages, to be involved in. Exactly the same ingredients that you would look for in all-age worship.

About twenty years ago my first book appeared. It was called *Tomorrow's People* and carried the sub-heading, 'A programme for involving young people in the life of the Church'. It was a very slim volume that offered 'possible ways of involving the youth of a parish – tomorrow's people of God – in the life of the Church'.

I can remember being very pleased, at the time, with the title. It now embarrasses me. It was condescending and, worst of all, it was theologically inaccurate. I would not dream of using such a title today, because, of course, our young people are, here and now, as much the people of God as we adults are.

Does that reflect that we have moved on in our understanding of the Church? Or was it just me that was blind at the time? (Interestingly no one else questioned the title, neither the editors or the book reviewers.) Are we now actively involved in all-age events because our appreciation of what being 'Church' means has evolved? Or, as one cynical vicar commented, 'We do it because we can't get Sunday school teachers any longer.' Experience of Church life suggests that we often find ourselves taking the correct course (further confirmation of the guidance of the Holy Spirit?) for the wrong reasons.

This is not a theological book, although inevitably there is a little theology to be found in it, because liturgy cannot be discussed without theology. It is not a complete handbook, because that is neither desirable nor possible. Like my other books it is a simple, practical book for busy pastors and their teams to dip into for a little guidance, support and encouragement. I hope that all Today's People of God will benefit from their efforts.

TONY CASTLE
Shrove Tuesday, 1994

INTRODUCTION
TO ALL-AGE EVENTS

THE GROWING IMPORTANCE OF ALL-AGE
EVENTS

Monks and nuns, Catholic and Anglican, along with Baptist ministers and Methodist lay preachers, Salvation Army officers and Orthodox priests, danced together at an Ecumenical Eucharist in Trafalgar Square, London, in May 1969. Millions witnessed the liturgical exuberance that Pentecost Sunday live on TV. The hundreds of Christians, of all traditions, who thronged the square that day felt that it was a new outpouring of the Holy Spirit. The Liturgical Movement, which had begun in the middle of the nineteenth century, had come of age.

The week-long festival of new forms of worship, which cumulated in the Trafalgar Square explosion of joy and unity, was aptly called 'That's the Spirit'. There were forty services using experimental forms of worship throughout the week in a dozen different central London churches, including St Martin in the Fields, the RC French Church in Leicester Square, the Baptist Tabernacle and the Methodist Central Hall, Westminster. Johnny Dankworth's jazz, with dance, poetry and revolutionary readings from Teilhard de Chardin, made for an exciting week. But all-age worship was not included or mentioned. We had not arrived, in 1969, at that important stage in the evolution of a pastoral liturgy.

What was experimental and exciting in 'That's the Spirit' is now commonplace. It is just a great pity that the promise of unity witnessed by the nation on TV that Pentecost Day has never been realised or witnessed in the same joyful way again.

As a member of the planning committee I know for sure that all-age worship was never mentioned at any of the committee's meetings, but in a sense it was presumed. It has always been a principle of Christian worship, although not always acted upon, that it is catholic. The marks of the Christian Church are the marks of its worship. As the Church is One, Holy, Catholic and Apostolic, so must be its worship.

All Christian worship has one principal aim and objective, to give adoration and praise to God the Father. It acknowledges the holiness of the One God and the intention of the Father that all his creatures should be holy.

It is the Christian community that worships, not a collection of individuals. Baptism unites all Christians in the one mystical Body of Christ; and it is Christ, the eternal High Priest, who ever lives to adore and intercede with the Father. Baptism is open to all, so the community of the baptized includes, equally, females and males; rich and poor; young and old; the married and the single; black and white. The Christian church is universal (catholic) in the sense that it is intended for all and can be found in every country.

There can be no authentic Christian church which is not apostolic, that is, founded upon the Apostles and their teaching. It is clear, from the New Testament, that this was the express wish and intention of Christ himself. The very first community 'devoted itself to the apostles' teaching and to the fellowship' (Acts 2:42).

Christian worship then must be One, Holy, Catholic and Apostolic. Naturally all-age worship is presumed in this, for all (catholic) must adore the One God (one) and receive strength to live the Christian life (holy) using the forms originating from the Apostles (apostolic).

Mention of the Apostles reminds us that the Church is itself apostolic, with a structure of authority and leadership founded upon and dating from the Apostles. Insights and guidance upon the nature of worship, particularly bearing upon all-age events, have been coming from Church authorities over the past thirty years. Here are but four of the numerous helpful insights from official documents.

The Liturgical Renewal of the past century began in the Roman Catholic Church and received great impetus, affecting all the main Western Christian Churches, from the documents issued by the Second Vatican Council. The Decree on the Liturgy, 1963, had this to say of the role of worship:

> The liturgy is the summit towards which the activity of the Church is directed; at the same time it is the fountain from which all her power flows.

The Church exists to worship. Important as activities like evangelisation and pastoral care are, they are secondary to the principal role of the Christian community. The secondary activities are nourished by good liturgy. This is obviously true if we think of the Euchartist or Lord's Supper. To obey the Lord by celebrating the sacred memorial meal in the community, is to spiritually feed and strengthen the same community.

The role of the minister is clearly spelt out in the same document:

> Ministers must realise that when the liturgy is cele-
> brated ... it is their duty to ensure that the congre-
> gation take part knowingly, actively and fruitfully.

If this paragraph had come from a Free or Nonconformist church source, perhaps a Congregational worship
authority, there would be little surprise. That it comes from
that Christian monolith which for centuries embodied
static rigidity in worship is amazing.

There are five important words in this short, illuminating passage.

- *Celebrated* Liturgy is a celebration. Humanly it is on a
  level with other social celebrations, like a birthday party,
  a wedding reception or anniversary celebration. The key
  note of all such 'celebrations' is joy. Liturgy should not
  be a staid and boring 'service'. (Perhaps it is time for us
  to abandon this word which has 'servitude' overtones).

- *Duty* Ministers may not, if they feel inclined, include the
  laity; they are obliged to do this, as a matter of duty. In
  other words, the role of minister includes involving the
  people in their community's act of worship.

- *Knowingly* There is much to know about the theology
  underlying Christian worship, besides its symbolism, language and history. Most members of congregations are
  not well informed. It is commonly agreed that the greatest need at this time is adult education in the Christian
  Faith.

- *Actively* The congregation is not an audience, nor is it

a group engaged in collective private prayer. It is the community of the baptized united with Christ, its head, giving adoration and praise to the Father. Each person has a right and a duty to be actively involved, and it is the minister's duty to ensure this happens. The many liturgical tasks, from welcoming to distributing hymn books, reading the lessons to taking the collection, need to involve as many of the congregation as possible. The minimum involvement would be joining in the prayers and the singing.

- *Fruitfully* A congregation that is taking part knowingly and actively is going to benefit and be enriched. One of the most observable results will be a growth in a sense of community, with the mutual support and encouragement which that brings.

The next quotation, from the same Decree of the Second Vatican Council, speaks for itself:

Worship should be distinguished by a noble simplicity; actions should be short, clear, and unencumbered by useless repetitions and should not require much explanation.

One of the most common complaints of young people is that Christian worship is boring. It need not be. There will be no place for boredom if a genuine effort is made to involve as many people, including the young people, as possible; if the worship has been prepared with 'celebration' in mind; if actions are short, clear and free of useless repetitions; and if all is conducted in 'a noble simplicity'.

While the above texts take all-age worship for granted, the Church of England report, 'The Child in the Church', 1976, sounds a warning to those who have neglected the place of children in the Christian community:

The Church that does not accept children uncon-
ditionally in its fellowship is depriving those children
of what is rightfully theirs, but the deprivation such as
the Church itself will suffer is far more grave.

In 1988 the General Synod Board of Education published the excellent 'Children in the Way' Report. It deserves
thoughtful reading from cover to cover and contains very
many quotable quotes. Here are two.

Particular worship events can move, refresh, stimulate,
feed or give insight. They are important and often
formative experiences no less for children as for
adults. Worship is an integral part of the life of faith,
in which the children, part of the faith community,
rightly participate. They too may experience the transcendent, find directions for thoughts and feelings
and share the cycle of festivals.

The acknowledgment of the merits of all-age worship is
clearly expressed. It is no longer assumed to be happening,
because, as 'The Child in the Church' report made clear,
a sufficient number of Christian communities had apparently neglected their young.
    Adults and children can learn so much from one another,
as this passage spells out:

Growing in faith also involves growing in worship. If
adults can, by example, help children to learn the
skills of worship – silence and concentration, the use
of symbol and ritual, the practice of prayer – then the

children can also bring their own particular capacities for worship.

The Faith community ignores the power of example at its peril. Thousands of converts have embraced Christianity through it. Albert Schweitzer once said, 'Example is not the main thing in influencing others – it is the only thing.' It is unnecessary to trace the evolution of a pastoral liturgy from Gueranger's work on Church music in 1830s, through the work of the Tractarians and the Ritualists, the input of Moody and Sankey and the efforts to reform the Book of Common Prayer, to the experimental worship of the 1960s and 'That's the Spirit'. It is quite evident that our knowledge, understanding and evaluation of worship is evolving. All-age worship and learning are very much part of that evolutionary process and it would be very bold to believe and state that we have arrived at the perfection of worship. As we can look back to the 1960s and see what has developed since then, so in thirty years time we or our successors will trace the further path of our pastoral liturgy. Changes in contemporary society are also powerful reasons for the growing importance of all-age events. Statistics are continually published which show the gradual break-up of the family as understood by Christians. The Churches need to be positively promoting the family and giving as much support as possible to single-parent families.

Paradoxically, as one after another newspaper article heralds the death of the family, more and more leisure centres and shopping malls are catering for family needs. While it is inevitable that the Church will follow, rather than set, trends in society, it should not be left behind. Why should families come to church and be split up into various departments? All-age events are, of course, not solely for families, there are many single people in our churches, including widows and widowers, who benefit when whole families are caught up in such events. The elderly are often 'rejuvenated' when sharing with the very young; the very young equally need the 'grandparent' dimension to human life. The local church community can supply many of the benefits of the extended family now largely lost in modern life.

All churches should be concerned that they are losing their young people; a glance round most congregations confirms that. The freshness of approach that all-age worship calls for breaks the formal mould of the regular church service and goes some way to answering the teenagers' charge that church services are boring. The only way to keep young people is to involve them in the action of the worship or the learning event.

The vitality and freshness of approach experienced all those years ago in Trafalgar Square, as the nation watched, could be recaptured in every local community, if the Holy Spirit is allowed to move and inspire, lead and encourage.

WHAT ARE ALL-AGE EVENTS?

The worship of the Christian Church, of whatever tradition, Orthodox, Catholic or Protestant, is God-directed and inclusive of the whole community. It is not for people of one race only, one gender only or one age only. It is for all.

However because it is framed so often by middle-aged males who have had the benefit of theological education, it so often, unintentionally, excludes many. Some adults, whose inadequate education finished at fifteen or sixteen, find the tone and language of some acts of worship alien to them. Children and young people share the same problem.

The emphasis in the epithet 'all-age' is upon 'all' and not upon 'age'. All-age events are inclusive not only of different age groups but also of people of different social backgrounds, education, etc. Those who interpret 'all-age' to mean adults with children have missed a very essential element.

An all-age event which caters only for middle-class parents with their children, in a locality where there is a broad social mix of people, is only being successful on one level. The same could be said of all white participants in a locality where there is a broad racial mix of people.

Here a word must be said about 'intention' and 'opportunity'. It must never be our intention to exclude anyone from any Christian event. That would not be in keeping with the love that Christ, who welcomed sinners and ate with them, expects of his followers. We should genuinely try to include and make welcome everyone of whatever social background, race or colour. This means advertising our events in places that we would not usually think of, eg the local fish and chip shop and newsagent, or giving out leaflets to the mothers waiting outside the local primary school at the end of the school day.

Constantly we must be offering people the opportunity to take part. Again and again the opportunity which we offer may be ignored or positively rejected, but that does not absolve us from continuing to offer it. The old saying 'Grace builds on nature' applies here. God's grace, in its own time, will work, if we do not tire of offering the opening.

All-age events are also about maturation in the Christian Faith. It is well known that just as each human person develops and matures physically and intellectually, so the same person develops morally and in faith.

It was in the sphere of moral development, through the influence of the research work of Piaget and Kohlberg, that work began on how humans develop religiously. Three educators, John Westerhoff, James Fowler and more recently Fritz Oser in Switzerland have shown that maturation in faith does not necessarily keep in step with the rest of the person's development. So a sixteen-year-old could be more mature in belief than a sixty-year-old.

Writing in the *Daily Mail*, in December 1993, I told how the students of sixteen that I teach enjoy questioning and discussing the real meaning of the Christmas stories found in Matthew and Luke. In a personal review and assessment of their work, 80 per cent had spoken of how much more deeply they understood and appreciated their Christian Faith as a result of the course. I received a number of confused and anxious letters from *Daily Mail* readers. One lady of sixty wrote, 'I am glad I had a simple upbringing to believe in Jesus. Without all this research. Do the young people believe in Jesus as their saviour? What on earth is the use of research into Scripture?' That devout lady would benefit from being with some of the young people.

The work of Westerhoff, Fowler and Oser, and the personal experience of those engaged in the religious education of young people and adults, make it quite clear that different age groups can benefit enormously from learning together, and worshipping together.

All-age events, embracing learning and worshipping, are occasions when people of every age, gender, and social and racial background have the opportunity of being together, sharing and growing, as the people of God. Such events develop a sense of community and assist each individual to move on to a higher stage of maturation in faith.

The above paragraph is something of a definition, answering succinctly the question, 'What are all-age events?' Perhaps we should 'unpack' it for a closer examination.

Churchgoing is not an insurance against final separation from God at the last judgment. It is possible to be a regular churchgoer and still fail to be taken up into heaven with the other sons and daughters of the Father. Jesus made it crystal clear in the parable of the Good Samaritan (Luke 10:27) and the Sheep and the Goats (Matthew 25:32) that loving God exclusively was insufficient in itself. Love must be balanced by and expressed through a love of neighbour. When asked 'Who is my neighbour?' Jesus replied with the good Samaritan story; in other words, 'everyone'.

In another place (Matthew 5:46) Jesus says, 'If you love those who love you, what reward will you get? ... And if you greet only your brothers, what are you doing more than others? Do not even pagans do that?'

Many Christians go to church, sit with their immediate family, talk with their friends and return home. Animosities may have been shelved and social prejudices not stirred, for personal peace of mind. But they may still lurk beneath the surface.

It is common for ministers and church leaders, of all churches, to feel that it is enough to get people to church, to fill the pews. That alone is not enough; it is a start. The building of 'community' is an essential requirement, so that the response to the second half of Christ's command can have an opportunity to grow and develop.

All-age learning and worshipping events, when people of all ages, genders, and social and racial backgrounds are involved with one another, are the ideal setting for Christian growth. Meeting others, sharing with others, learning to accept one another in love, growing together in the Faith, fulfils the totality of Christ's new commandment. And he is present.

The development of the local faith community, as a community, and the growth in faith of its individual members, must be in keeping with the will of God.

THE CHURCH AS FAMILY

The Church has changed and is changing. Christians do not live in some kind of holy vacuum, apart from and uninfluenced by the multitude of forces at play in society. The change started during the Industrial Revolution when society started to change. And the changing has not stopped. No longer do we simply have town and country parishes or church communities. The church in a scattered rural area may have a minister or priest serving three or four tiny communities, with few children and many retired folk. A suburban church may have a thriving community with a good balance of all-age groups. And an inner-city parish may have a tiny number at the weekend and worker-worshippers during weekday lunchtimes. There are almost as many different types of community as there are different kinds of environment.

For the first time in history most of the population are mobile, symbolised by the popular birthday present for seventeen-year-olds of a driving lesson, or programme of lessons. So worshippers can pick and choose where and with whom they will worship.

Given the nature of some environments many people no longer feel a part of their local neighbourhood communities (if any sense of community exists at all) and they experience 'community' at their place of work or with leisure-time companions.

The apparent growth in lawlessness in society has resulted in an increasing number of people who 'keep themselves to themselves' and become ever more isolated behind security devices. This isolation is so foreign to the human spirit that security from exterior threats causes interior desolation and despair.

Within this ever-changing society, like the stillness at the eye of the storm, part of it but apart from it, is the Body of Christ, the Church, the community of the baptized, who are 'in the world but not of the world' (John 17:16). People need one another; they need to belong to 'community' for their physical, emotional and spiritual good health. The risen Christ provides for this need in those committed to him; being 'church' is an essential part of being 'Christian'. No one can be a Christian alone and in isolation.

There is a wonderful icon from Russia, created by the famous icon painter of the fifteenth century, Andrei Rublev. It depicts the three visitors, who according to Genesis chapter 18 called upon Abraham, 'near the great trees of Mamre'. The text opens with the words, 'The Lord appeared to Abraham...' then speaks of 'three men standing nearby'.

Rublev skilfully and beautifully leads those who sit meditatively before the icon into a consideration of the family of the Holy Trinity. The unity of love is symbolised by the circular structure of the icon. The inclination of the figures' bodies and heads, the facial expression and costumes all suggest a bond of love between them. The 'motion' of the icon, the way the viewer's eye is drawn around the group, from right to left, is towards the 'Father'.

Christian teaching has always understood that the human family with its bond of love is but a poor shadow of the 'family' of the Holy Trinity (Ephesians 3:15).

Different 'models' have been proposed for the Church: 'the people of God', 'God's pilgrim people', etc. That which springs most naturally to mind, especially since baptism in 'the name of the Father and of the Son and of the Holy Spirit' makes all the baptized brothers and sisters in the Lord, is the Church as the family of God. Presumably because the title 'sister' and 'brother' had, in the past, been adopted in political circles, there has been an uneasiness about using these titles in the Church today as they once were in the early Church. 'Suppose a brother or sister is without clothes and daily food...' (James 2:15).

'Family worship' seems a good practical title for all-age worship, as long as we understand what we mean by 'family'. Not in society's understanding of the modern nuclear family of mother, father and child(ren) or even in the more traditional concept of the extended family, but in the Christian sense that we all, regardless of age or gender, are members of God's family.

There remains a problem. Unless people are going to be regularly reminded of this (and is that practical?), the title 'Family worship' can be felt by some to be excluding. As Esther de Waal has said, in *Seeking God*:

It should be honestly admitted that the image so often conjures up a picture of young marrieds with young children, a model that excludes and thereby wounds the majority of the human race. Those who are single, those who are part of a broken or dispersed family, depend upon the warmth and support that comes from friendship.

So while we should think 'family' when we talk of and work with our Christian community, and treat one another with the respect due to a brother or sister, that title for our worship is inappropriate – unless, of course, it really is a special service for young families. Just as in schools teachers can no longer assume that most pupils in the class come from a traditional family, so too in church life and worship no such assumptions can be made.

SEASONAL OPPORTUNITIES

A BBC television programme on the family concluded that Christmas is a woman's festival. If it were not for mothers, wives, grandmothers and sisters, Christmas would not exist as it does. While the menfolk are entrusted with purchasing and bringing in the Christmas tree, most of the shopping, card-writing, decorating, and so on are done by the women-folk. Why? The programme suggested that women imitate and repeat what their mothers have traditionally done; because that is what has always been done and, where appropriate, for the sake of the children and family unity.

The 'family' of the church community imitates and repeats in much the same way. Tradition rules in some church communities. That can be a strength, but it can also be a weakness. Continuity and familiarity in the 'family' of the parish or church are important just as they are in the individual home. They strengthen a sense of belonging, ownership and unity with past generations. However they can be a weakness because they can stifle understanding, fresh ideas and creativity. There is a danger that the same aging clique of church members will possessively control 'what has always been done'.

If such a situation exists it is not easily remedied, as those who have experienced it know. It is only too easy to offend a dedicated and long-serving group of helpers. One way of working a change is to include the principal leader or leaders in a large team of people who are planning an event. Members of this team can suggest new ideas and encourage discussion on them, so that all are involved.

Another way is to find new areas for visual aids, decoration, and so on and bring in different groups to take responsibility. For example, if the original body of workers has always worked on the window ledges, another parish association or perhaps the young people could use the pillars, or the pew ends.

It has already been emphasised that the primary purpose and direction of worship is the adoration of God. However, as Christian worship is incarnational, that is, it is offered to God the Father through our eternal High Priest, the Word made flesh, who as man can share and sympathise with our weakness, it also fulfils a deep-felt human need. While Jesus did not need to seek forgiveness, he implored it for others ('Father forgive them, they do not know what they are doing' – Luke 23:34) and was totally aware of our need to offer it and receive it. (Was it not he who taught us the words, 'Forgive us our sins, as we forgive those who sin against us'?)

It was Christ Jesus, too, who told us to 'ask ... seek ... knock ... and the door will be opened to you' (Matthew 7:7). Petition should be followed by thanksgiving, the very name for the central act of worship, the Eucharist. This is

the supreme act of Christian thanksgiving, so named
from the very earliest times.

All of these, adoration, penitence, intercession and
thanksgiving, have their place in each act of worship and in
the Christian year.

Starting with the penitential season of Advent with its
four weeks of preparation for the wonder, adoration and
thanksgiving of Christmas, the cycle of the year unfolds.
Every year reveals the whole mystery of Christ, not only
from his incarnation and birth, until his ascension, but
also the day of Pentecost and the expectation of his blessed,
hoped-for return in glory.

Easter is the pivot and pinnacle of that year. We are the
Easter People, followers of the risen Christ who have been
baptized into his death and resurrection. Just as the central
focus of our year is the Christian Passover, so weekly on
the first day of the week, the day of the Resurrection, we
gather to commemorate and draw strength from the central mystery of our faith. Whether we are celebrating
Sunday or Christmas Day, we are celebrating the presence
of the risen Lord among us. All Christian worship is resur-
rection-centred; and while the Christian seasons come and
go, all events either look forward or back to Easter.

All-age events are ideally suited for the seasonal celebrations of the Christian family.

During Advent everyone is preparing in one way or
another for Christmas; this uniting activity can be capital-
ised upon. While Christmas can be a lonely time for single
people and the elderly living alone, this in itself creates a
challenge for a caring community. At the very least such
a community can mount a 'neighbourhood watch' over
the Christmas period, which can involve all ages.

Preparing for Easter, by using the season of Lent, could

involve a programme for the whole parish or church community. Imaginatively and energetically the hour following
the principal Sunday act of worship could include refresh-
ments with a simple, encompassing-all learning activity,
orientated to the message of Easter.

Easter is not only important, it must be seen by the
whole community to be important. If there is to be no
special all-age event, then at the very least everyone must
'experience' the Easter worship as of vital significance;
Christmas should not out-shine it. Those who plan the
liturgy for the day can make a special effort to involve even
more of the community, of all ages and conditions of life,
than usual in the celebration.

As no one can believe or live the Christian life without
the gift of the Holy Spirit, Pentecost is a most suitable time
for an all-age event. It is also important because, of the
three major festivals of the Christian year, this tends to be
the most ignored and neglected of them. (The confusion
with the national Whitsun, or Spring, Bank holiday doesn't
help.)

PLANNING FOR ALL-AGE EVENTS

Once the decision has been made to try or expand into
an all-age event, the next step is to form a team of people
who will be responsible for all aspects of the event. No
matter how gifted a pastoral leader may be, or how experienced, a team is necessary, for these reasons:

1. One person is going to be, obviously, male or female,
   and from a particular age group. Even with the best of
   intentions she or he will not fully know and be seen to

represent the interests of the other sex or other age groups.

2. A wide range of expertise is required which no one person is likely to embrace. For example, an excellent musician may not be sufficiently artistic or energetic to produce the posters and advertising required.

3. The work load can be considerable and this needs to be shared.

4. During the planning the insights of a team of enthusiastic people are going to be of wider benefit than the good ideas of an individual. Some of the best ideas come from the most unexpected quarters.

5. Every event should be reviewed afterwards, so that lessons can be learnt and improvement made for next time. This can only take place efficiently if there is a team of people.

Choosing the team requires careful thought. We are dealing here with ideals and one may have to settle for realistic alternatives.

The team leader may or may not be the minister or priest. This depends on how the pastoral leader sees his role and on his own gifts and talents. Being a clergyman does not necessarily equate with being a good team leader.

After a leader, the team wants, above all else, balance. While not all ages have to be represented, there needs to be a child (say about twelve) and a young person in the later teens. A mix of married and single people needs to be included and a balance of male and female.

A musician, or someone acquainted with current church music, a good storyteller and someone who is a good administrator would be assets. A group of about six (maximum of eight) would be ideal.

In recruiting the team do not advertise for volunteers. The team should be chosen and invited to belong. If possible choose those who are not already committed to jobs in the church community.

Once the team has been put together, before it starts planning an event, a quiet two to three hour training session together is a good idea. Some dioceses have specialists trained in liturgy and in all-age activities, and they are often delighted to lead an introductory training session. You will be able to talk over the specific needs of your church family with them.

There may be the natural temptation to skimp the preparations and planning, but it is important to resist such a temptation. Every home decorator knows that the better the cleaning down, sanding, and filling before the painting, the better the final result. It is exactly the same here. In choosing a team and training them you are building well for the future.

At the first meeting of the team to plan an all-age event, explore what you are setting out to achieve. These or similar questions might be usefully explored.

Are we planning a learning event or an act of worship?
Or is it to be a learning event leading on to an act of worship?
Why do we want to hold this all-age event?
What do we hope will be the end result? What is our aim?
How much time will we give to it? Will it be for an hour or an afternoon? A whole day or a weekend?
Will it replace our usual Sunday act of worship or be in addition to it?
Who do we hope to interest? Our usual congregation?

Those who occasionally attend? Those who belong
to the wider community?

Should we invite another faith community to join us?
Another community of our own tradition? Or is this
an opportunity for practical ecumenism?

Who will lead the event? Do we need a co-ordinator
or a guest speaker?

Do we need more than one leader – one for the
learning part and one for the worship?

How will we structure the event? Will there be a
speaker, then workshops? Will it be theme-based?

Do we need to check that the hall, meeting or committee rooms are free at the time we need them?

How much will the event cost? How shall we fund it?
Can we make a small charge or will the church carry
the cost?

Do we need to book or loan any equipment such as a
video recorder, monitor, OHP?

What effective methods, beyond the usual ones, will
we use to advertise the event?

Are we all prepared to put in the time and effort
required to make the event a success?

Once the aim of the event has been clarified, there are
a number of key guiding points to keep in mind.

1. Allow plenty of time for planning and preparations;
for example the initial meeting for a Lent programme
should ideally take place before Christmas. Realistically
that is unlikely to happen. However the team must be
called together immediately after Epiphany.

2. From the very outset the team members should be
encouraged to talk to the wider community about the

coming event, making it quite clear that it is not planned for children, or specially for families; it's an every-
people's event. Once the wrong idea gets sounded
abroad it is difficult to correct it.

3. From the beginning it is important to involve others
in the preparations – children especially. The young
people should not get the idea that the adults are
putting something on for them!

4. Design your own programme or order of service, no
matter how simple. In these days of desktop publishing
there must be someone in the community who would
be pleased to help with this. Simple does not mean
slipshod: it can be made attractive with the use of clip-
art books. (A few simple examples of this are included
in the appendix, but there are many such books on
the market.) In an order of service give no alternatives; the order of service should flow easily straight
through.

5. When planning an act of worship, look for a theme in
the Gospel reading for the day, or at least in keeping
with the readings. Choose hymns and prayers that
relate to and illumine the theme. (It is a good idea to
inform the congregation of the theme, at the beginning, if it is not spelt out in the order of service sheet.)

6. While there is a problem about 'sacred language' (as
we discuss later), the minister, priest or worship leader
should not give way to the temptation of explaining
everything in the service. Most of the time the liturgy
should be allowed to speak for itself.

7. Maintain a balance between the old and the new, familiarity and novelty. Variety keeps worship vibrant and
fresh, but people need the security too of a familiar
structure and established framework.

8. Television has conditioned people to expect a 'mosaic' rather than a continuous 'seamless robe'. You could for example, use several readers in a part-reading or a dramatised version rather than one voice, as well as breaking up activities and inserting short texts or readings.

9. Capitalise on people's talents. The most surprising gifts can be used.

10. The significance of practical activities is not always immediately obvious to the participants. Reflection upon them is necessary to draw out their meaning and purpose.

WATCH YOUR LANGUAGE!

Each discipline and profession has its own special language. The banking world uses terms not found in the local hospital; insurance companies and the Inland Revenue use a language that ordinary mortals grapple with. Those who have returned to teaching in the last year or two have discovered a totally new vocabulary in the staff room, which takes weeks to learn and use confidently.

It is no different in the Church. It is an institution with its own 'restricted code'. Just as outsiders feel alien in a banking, hospital or school situation, so too do many who attend a church service only rarely. While this is true of adults it is even more true of children and young people.

If a Rip Van Winkle adolescent from the 'fifties woke up in the 'nineties he or she would find it hard to converse with today's teenagers. Television-speak and computer jargon, along with the corruption of simple English words, would render any conversation difficult. Besides the obvious example, like being unable to use the word 'gay' to mean happy and joyful, there has been some Americanisation and other words have dropped out of use.

Experienced Christian educators know that nothing can be taken for granted. We are not talking here of theological words, like incarnation, redemption, justification. These are definitely inaccessible to modern young people, and to most adults. Worship leaders would hopefully know this. Here we are referring to words and terms which are used repeatedly in church but are no longer understood, terms like 'the ministry of Christ' (something to do with the Government?), 'the passion of Christ' (something to do with romance, with sexual overtones?).

One reason why we are losing young people from the Church is that they find services boring, which in part springs from a sense of alienation due to the unfamiliarity of much of the vocabulary.

An all-age planning team should look for an opportunity to discuss 'sacred' language and the care that should be taken over inclusive language. Attitudes to the latter should be reasonable and just, without being rampantly feminist, or anti-feminist. It would be somewhat contradictory to make every effort to include everyone in the community in an all-age event, then thoughtlessly use exclusive language.

2

ALL-AGE WORSHIP

WORSHIP

Worship, as we have already noted in the Introduction, is only given to God, as Father, through the Son, in the power of the Holy Spirit; for 'by the Spirit we cry, "Abba", Father' (Romans 8:15). And again in Ephesians Paul reminds us that 'through him (Christ) we have access to the Father by one spirit' (2:14).

From the earliest years of Christianity the word 'liturgy' has been used to describe the worship of the Christian community. The word actually comes from two Greek words *laos* meaning 'people' and *ergon*, 'work'. There is a very important idea hidden there. The liturgy is not the work of the professional clergy and ministers, with the people present as onlookers. The liturgy is the work of the people, that community to which we are all equally called to belong, regardless of age, sex or social class.

In the house-churches of the first century of the Church everyone of all ages, classes and races could fully participate. In his first letter to the Christians at Corinth Paul takes them to task for splitting into cliques. The rich, for example, were not sharing with the poor. The norm is participation by all (1 Corinthians 11:17–22).

Lay participation in the Church's worship probably started to decline when the Eucharist had to be celebrated in the secrecy of the catacombs. Much later in the Middle Ages the hundreds of monasteries throughout Europe exerted a very strong influence upon church architecture and design. The choir stalls, still to be seen in our ancient English cathedrals, were set apart from the people, between the officiating priest and the congregation. Cut off from the liturgy by a rood screen the people could hardly see what was going on, let alone participate. The rood screens came down in the Reformation period, but by then class barriers had gone up in society. By Victorian times worship had become very formal and, of course, children were expected to be seen but not heard.

The Liturgy Movement would now appear to have brought us full circle. All-age worship is as close as the Church has been for 1,800 years to the expected norms of the first and second century.

It might be a useful exercise for the all-age worship team to research the above ideas a little more fully, as part of their training.

CHARACTERISTICS OF ALL-AGE WORSHIP

What were the characteristics of first-century Christian worship, when 'they broke bread in their homes and ate together with glad and sincere hearts' (Acts 2:46)?

The simple description reminds one of a wedding reception or banquet (did they have the Messianic banquet in mind, while celebrating?). The celebration of a wedding brings together people of a wide range of ages and backgrounds; it is a fairly adult occasion but efforts are made to incorporate the children and young people. When there is dancing, grandparents dance with teenagers and parents with childen, it is a truly 'family' occasion.

What prompts ordinary, everyday people who read the tabloids to have 'glad and sincere hearts'? It is no great mystery, as is clear when crowds gather on holiday, when they are free of everyday cares and anxieties. I described in the Introduction a holiday where 'the ingredients were lively music, plenty of encouragement to participate, good confident leadership and simple actions for people of all ages to be involved in'.

Such ingredients do not necessarily suggest 'free' worship, they can be totally in keeping with liturgy that is ritually structured. Interestingly, it would appear that the worship of the Free or Nonconformist churches has, in many places, become more structured and rigid in form with the passing of the years. At the same time the liturgy of, for example, the Roman Catholic Church has become more relaxed, less structured and more involving. It is customary in several of the 'Free' churches for the minister to choose the theme of the service, the readings, the hymns, and prepare a sermon. At the service itself it is assumed that the same minister will do everything himself, read the lessons from Scripture, announce the hymns, lead the prayers and, of course, preach. Modern Roman Catholics, attending such a service, are amazed to find that the lay people are so little involved, when they themselves are accustomed to considerable involvement in the act of worship.

The term 'lively music' does not suggest any particular style or type of music. Most styles can be 'lively' if carefully chosen for the occasion and played wth zest and commitment. (I say 'play' rather than 'perform' because too often

musicians, and choirs too, can put on 'a performance'.)
Music in the setting of worship is a ministry. Those who
proclaim the word of God as readers fulfil a ministry, as
do the musicians and the choir.

A choir can be injurious to good liturgy. The great St
Augustine of Hippo is credited with the saying, 'He who
sings prays twice.' The object of the music is not just to
dignify worship, valid as this is, but to unify the worshipping
community in song, in praying twice. If the congregation
is inhibited by the choir and is tending to leave the singing
to them, then the role and even the future of the choir
should be carefully examined. There is no need to have a
choir, simply because there has always been one.

No congregation is 'encouraged to participate' if the
professionals – the priest or minister(s) and the choir –
appear to have it all sewn up between them. It is simplicity
itself to creep into the church, find a quiet corner, observe
and listen, nod to the sidesman as you return the unused
hymn book at the door, and slip away.

First, everyone in the worshipping community needs to
know and understand that worship is about participating;
it is not collective private prayer. Then the people could
be encouraged to arrive a little early, so that there is time
to chat and begin to 'feel' like a community gathering to
worship together. (If this offends those who like to have a
period of quiet before the service it can take place outside
– weather permitting – in the porch or some other desig-
nated area.) Next an 'animator' may be used to introduce
the theme of the service before it starts, giving a general
welcome to newcomers, encouraging all to sing, etc. The
person to fulfil such a lively, positive role has to be carefully
chosen; more harm than good can result from the choice
of an insensitive or abrasive character.

The planning team can explore with the priest or minister how this preparation can best be carried forward into the service, this leads us to the next important element, 'confident leadership'.

Some ideas for simple actions, from processions to drama and dance, are suggested in later sections.

MUSIC

More than 30,000 Christian hymns, all known and studied by hymnologists, have come down to us from the early centuries of Christianity and the Middle Ages.

The great majority are now unusable because they express the Christian mystery in the thought patterns, style and language of the period in which they were written. Each age has felt the need to express its worship in song according to its own needs and insights, and from its own social setting. There is little value then in using hymns and songs of the Victorian period, beyond the comfort of familiarity, one hundred or more years later.

In all-age worship, particularly, we must take care to inspect the words of the hymns we select. Choosing old favourites simply because they are popular with some (perhaps even an influential part of the congregation) will not do. (Some churches have the occasional 'Songs of Praise' service when they sing all the old favourites, without any concern about the theme of the service, the actual words, or the theology expressed in the hymns.)

With the passing of time words change their meaning. Take for example the word 'awful'. When included in old hymns it meant 'full of awe' or 'inspiring reverence'. To a modern person it means 'terrible' or 'horrid', and gives quite the wrong image of God.

Again social and cultural changes render concepts, phrases and terms meaningless or out of tune with a modern view of life. The military might of the British Army of Victorian times with its resplendent uniforms (an army which did not fight once between 1815 and 1853) inspired many Victorian hymn writers to use military metaphors and terms in their hymns. (It is no coincidence that that inspiring band of socially minded Christians who were founded at this time, the Salvation Army, followed the same pattern, with their officers, citadels, etc.) 'Onward Christian soldiers', for example, reflects the triumphalism of the late Victorian period. There was no television then to bring the horrors of war into the ordinary person's lounge. We have seen several horrific war experiences since then; military images are no longer uplifting and inspiring.

Another example, and there is no lack of them, is 'For all the saints', which contains many such triumphant concepts. Do modern young people respond to the image of Jesus as 'their captain in the well fought fight'?

Our choice of music is important. Children and young people can share fully in the singing (and continue unselfconsciously bursting into song during the week) long before they can understand the sermon or the prayers of the service. The music and hymns must therefore be selected to support, reflect or develop the theme of the service. Those choosing the music should have a clear understanding of the function of music and its relevance to the service. This requires proper communication and open discussion with all those involved in the planning. Church music does not exist to please the musicians, the choir or a music group. It is not a platform for showing off talent and virtuosity. Liturgical music is at the service of the people of God as they adore and serve God.

Music can be used in many different ways in an act of worship:

1. Instrumental music before or after the service.
2. Accompaniment for the singing of hymns, choruses, etc. by the congregation.
3. Accompaniment for a soloist or the choir.
4. Background music during a Scripture reading, a dramatic presentation or choral speaking.
5. Accompaniment for liturgical movement or dance.

People sometimes assume that the organ is more appropriate for older folk and traditional congregational singing, and the guitar is right for youngsters. But it's not that simple. For one thing, 'playing' the organ, the piano or the guitar is not the same as 'leading' the singing. A good organist or pianist does not necessarily know how to lead good congregational singing. A different style of playing is required; one that leads and gives support to the peoples' voices.

Exactly the same applies to a guitar or guitarists. The guitar alone, especially an acoustic guitar, is unsuitable for leading good singing. Another instrument like a double bass, or a glockenspiel, is needed to give ground support to the guitar, add volume and give the firmness and clarity necessary to accompany congregational singing effectively.

It is the style of the music and the setting of the occasion which suggests the type of accompaniment, not the constitution of the congregation. Organ music is quite acceptable to the majority of young people, and quite a lot of the elderly enjoy hearing and being accompanied by guitars.

Nor should one jump to the conclusion that choruses are everyone's cup of tea. The traditional approach to church music has always been to use a mix of old and new and that still remains a sound approach.

Apart from appreciating the excellence of beautifully performed music, appreciation is at its highest when participating oneself. We must never forget that we are considering the use of music in the worship of God, who considers the intentions of the heart more than the skill of hand, voice or ear.

The planning group might like to consider the implications of the following simple story from France.

A French monastery was well known in its province for its hospitality and generous practical help for the poor. However when it came to sing the Divine Office in the church there was not one monk who could sing well to lead the others, but they did their best. Try as they would the music in their services was always a failure.

One day a travelling monk, a great singer, asked for and was given hospitality. Great was the community's delight, for now they could have much more worthy worship. They talked among themselves and hoped that they could keep him with them always.

But that night an angel came to the abbot in a dream. 'Why was there no music in your chapel tonight? We always listen for the beautiful music that rises from your services.'

'You must be mistaken,' replied the abbot. 'Usually we have no music worth listening to; but tonight we had a trained singer with a wonderful voice. For the first time in all these years our music was beautiful.'

The angel smiled. 'And yet up in heaven we heard nothing,' he said softly.

THE USE OF POP MUSIC

Everything that makes up the daily pattern and content of
daily life – unless of course it is sinful – can be considered
for use in worship. The Incarnation teaches us that the
sacred and secular are not apart and separate. As God
was in man redeeming the world, so we seek God in our
neighbour and the sacred in the secular. As Gerald Manley
Hopkins put it:

The world is charged with the grandeur of God.
It will flame out, like shining from shook foil...

Fired with this appreciation, in the late 'sixties and early
'seventies writers who were familiar with popular music
encouraged its use in religous education and worship. Such
writers as Tony Jasper, and publishers like Galliard, offered
ideas on how pop music could and should be used to
praise God and make the Church more relevant for
modern young folk. Back in 1973 I wrote, in *Tomorrow's
People*:

Why 'pop' you might ask. Isn't it loud, cheap and
often debasing? Of course, it can be and sometimes it
is, but often it is elevating and thought-provoking. The
term 'pop music' covers such a vast field, and in a way
reflects all the subtle variations in life itself. Side by
side, like neighbours in a street, you can have, in the
Pop Charts, a sermonette presenting all the qualities
required for a holy life, and a very suggestive and
crude love song. It is for us to use the good, and reject
the bad, and so we are not only on the same wave-

length as our young people, but we also help them to develop their own critical faculty.

The pop scene has changed considerably since those words were penned. At about that time songs like, 'Bridge over Troubled Water', 'My Sweet Lord', 'I'd like to teach the world to sing' and 'Amazing Grace' were at the top of the charts. These and others were used in worship with young people.

At first sight the pop music of the 'nineties may not appear to be such a fruitful source of material. But today's young people can and do draw on their contemporary music scene as they worship God. And 'alternative' worship services have made imaginative use of the contemporary pop scene.

Phil Collins has recorded some usable material, e.g. 'Another Day in Paradise'. There's also Wet, Wet, Wet's 'I get by with a little help from my friends', and groups like U2 have some good useful recordings.

Experience has shown, however, that pop music is often inappropriate for use in the average church service. It can however be of real value in special services, particularly if these are not taking place in the church or are part of an all-age learning event.

The term 'pop music' covers a vast range from Acid House to the Country and Western style. Popular classical pieces find their way into the charts along with Rap; almost anything goes. Here 'pop music' means those tracks that are widely known because they have figured prominently in the pop charts. For our purposes they can be divided into two main types.

The first type, rare these days, is those which have a direct religious content and message. These can be used as they are, with no necessary explanation before or after use. Examples of this type, which are nearly all 'golden oldies', are 'My Sweet Lord' by George Harrison, and 'Amazing Grace'.

The second type, the more numerous, are those pieces of music which may be used with an 'applied' meaning. That is, they were not written with any religious or spiritual content, but the words and sentiments of the song can be understood, with explanation, in a religious context. Reference has already been made to the old favourite of Simon and Garfunkel, 'Bridge Over Troubled Waters'. Other examples of the same vintage are James Taylor's 'You've Got a Friend', several by the ever popular group, Abba, and 'Everything I do, I do for you' by Bryan Adams.

Pop music is most effective if used with proper preparation, in the right setting and sparingly. To use it too often is to blunt its impact, while to consider its use once in a while is to link worship with everyday life. It can demonstrate, particularly to the young at heart, that Christian learning and worship are not an isolated part of life but integrated, incarnationally, with the rest.

Moreover if a particular piece of music is shown to have a connecting link with spiritual or moral values, then each time people hear it in their own homes or places of work or leisure, the spiritual message drawn from it may be recalled to their minds.

In an all-age event pop music can be used for discussion purposes, to illustrate a teaching point, or as a stimulus for meditation.

The challenge for the planning team is to be imaginative and creative, yet sensitive, in exploring ways to relate external truths to today's culture.

MOVEMENT AND DANCE

Dance before the Lord? David did (2 Samuel 6:14–16) – and his snobby wife objected. 'Lacking in dignity,' she said.

Which of the two was right – David or Michal? Which pleased the Lord? Is it helpful to praise God in song and dance, as the psalmist says (Psalms 149:3)? Or are movement and dance something best left to people whose culture finds natural expression in the dance?

In the West we tend to associate dance either with the National Ballet, or with gyrations on the floor of the local discotheque or night club. It is either highly skilled and professional or it has erotic overtones. Neither would seem to recommend movement and dance to church usage.

It is through our bodies, however, that we relate to other people, to the world around us and to God. That is why we need a liturgy.

In his self-revelation God respects our humanity. He did not send an angel or a book – he sent his Son. God became human to reach more humans more fully. This self-communication continues in the liturgy and we respond with the whole of our being, bodies and all. Thus it involves movement as well as stillness, speech and song as well as silence.

The practical question is more difficult: when and how to move? A good place to start is where we are. Movement is already a part of our worship, in processions, the sign of peace, etc. Why not develop and improve what already takes place? For example, processions can be a great success in all-age events. An enthusiastic letter by the Rev. Mike Sheffield, parish priest of Swanmore, Ryde, Isle of Wight, offers some ideas:

Processions of different kinds have become a great 'hit' in the monthly Family Eucharists. We have followed a donkey on Palm Sunday; walked around the churches looking at stained glass windows; processed around the parish streets linking our two churches; and moved with the children to different places within the buildings for different parts of the service. This helps to keep their interest, and can be an opportunity for teaching. For example, at the font we stopped and prayed for all who had been baptized in the church, and at the main door we thought of the times we just 'walked past God' and therefore made our confession.

These ideas are simple and none of them new. But simplicity is often best and we who have been promoting liturgical practice for many years have to remember that new generations keep coming along (while inertia on our part may set in) to whom these are new and exciting ways of being involved.

Associating movement with vocal public prayer has likewise a great value, even though it too is not new.

These illustrations of a dance/movement sequence to the Lord's Prayer and the Gloria were devised by Gillian Martlew. It is intended that they flow in uninterrupted sequence depicting the basic human response to God.

Our Father,

Who art in heaven,

hallowed be thy name.

Thy kingdom come.
Thy will be done
on earth, as it is in heaven.

Give us this day our
daily bread,

and forgive us our trespasses,

as we forgive those who
trespass against us,

and lead us not into
temptation,

But deliver us from evil.

Glory to God in
the highest,
and peace to his
people on earth.

Lord God, heavenly King,
almighty God and Father,

we worship you,
we give you thanks,
we praise you for your glory.

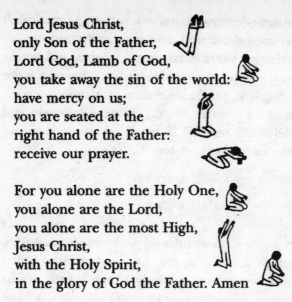

Lord Jesus Christ,
only Son of the Father,
Lord God, Lamb of God,
you take away the sin of the world:
have mercy on us;
you are seated at the
right hand of the Father:
receive our prayer.

For you alone are the Holy One,
you alone are the Lord,
you alone are the most High,
Jesus Christ,
with the Holy Spirit,
in the glory of God the Father. Amen

Dramatic movement, either as mime or straight-forward acting, can wonderfully enhance the liturgy of the Word. There are many books of Scripture-based plays which give ideas, (see Appendix for suggested books). It can also be very effective to ask a small group of people to work on a Psalm, or other suitable Bible reading, and to create movements and gestures to reflect and illustrate its meaning. A reading accompanied in this way can make a great impact.

Where the movement is not a simple mime accompanying a straight-forward story, it is probably best for the movement to follow after the reading. It will then serve to illustrate God's Word in a way which allows people to absorb the message of the text more slowly and to meditate on it in their own way. Movement is used here to stimulate the graced imagination.

Dance, as distinct from movement, is a delicate issue, not

from the theoretical point of view, but from the practical, It is wonderful when done well, and distracting and embarrassing when done badly. Well meaning girls and young women leaping around in glossy leotards can become more absorbed in displaying their skills than in prompting spiritual meditation on a Scripture text. Professional help and advice are definitely needed if an all-age event is to use dance as a medium of expression.

PUPPETS

Puppets can convey powerful and memorable messages. They can assume a reality in the eyes of those who watch and those who use them regularly which hardly seems possible. Observe an audience of young children watching a live performance of Sooty and Sweep, they are totally caught up in the reality of it all. The creator of Sooty, Harry Corbett, was so involved with his creation that he used to drill air-holes in the puppet's travelling box!

Mention 'puppets' and people immediately assume that you are talking about entertainment for children. After all, aren't all puppets, like Sooty and Sweep, Punch and Judy, solely for children? Experienced puppeteers insist that this is not so. Well over half of their audiences, they say, are adults. While a performance appears to be for children, adults watch with their guard down; while the children enjoy the storyline, the adults appreciate the nuances of the more subtle message.

What is a puppet? The classical definition is much wider than most people would expect. It is virtually any representation or image that stands for another person, whether or not it uses gloves or strings.

The use of puppets in evangelism has a long Christian history. There is evidence that they were used to teach with in the catacombs in the first centuries of Christianity. The familiar Punch and Judy shows originated from a Christian background. It was originally the Adam and Eve show, but when this became offensive to the Church authorities, the presentation became more secularised. With the influence of the Italian puppeteers of the seventeenth century and a comic character called Pulchinella, the Punch and Judy show was born.

In the Middle Ages, in the processions celebrating Christian festivals and saints days, giant puppets, twice life-size, were held aloft. They were little more than a representation of a person, attached to a pole and held high as the procession wound its way through a city.

Modern Christian puppeteers have found that a puppet show is a disarming and non-threatening method of proclaiming Christ's Good News in a public place, like the beach at Blackpool or any other seaside resort.

Puppets can be used in all-age events in several ways. One of the community's worship-leaders, such as the priest or minister, deacon or one of the planning team, might like to explore this medium of communication further and become an amateur puppeteer. Puppeteers often work in pairs, one handling the puppet(s) and one being the 'straight' man, so that a conversation, debate or argument can take place between the two.

The church community's worship team might consider inviting a Christian professional (in the sense of more skilled, rather than earning a living from it), to come and lead a service or a workshop. This could make the basis of a very happy and productive day or half-day.

Flowing out of this event, or organised separately, the

children and young people, with parents and other interested adults, could have a 'Make a Puppet' session. They could then use the puppets to retell selected parables or events from the New Testament.

There are four basic types of puppet that can be made by anyone, very simply and inexpensively.

1. *Large puppets*: A long pole, like a broomstick, is required with a stick or rod as a cross-piece to represent the shoulders. Arms may or may not be added. A head of papier-mache attached to the top of the pole with a smock-like piece of material hanging from the horizontal shoulders. The head and clothes can be changed for different characters.

2. *Paper plate puppets*: A white paper plate, with a stick attached as a handle, can be turned into a mask. A character can be drawn on the plate and the voice behind the mask can make it a 'talking head'. Again these can be used to act out a parable or Gospel incident.

3. *String puppets*: These require more work and patience to make and are particularly suited to representing animals, like dogs, horses, dragons. Using disused plastic washing-up liquid bottles, lengths of string and two short pieces of wood, to which the strings are attached for control, animals can be made for use in story telling.

4. *Glove puppets*: As the name suggests, a redundant and adapted glove is used, and these can be more suitable than string puppets to represent people. The index finger fits into a 'head' and the thumb and second finger become the arms. There are other adaptations and the heads can be interchangeable.

STORYTELLING

Everyone loves a good story. As followers of the greatest and most famous of all storytellers we should make greater use of story. Storytelling crosses all age, sex, race and social barriers.

Jesus told his stories to all-age groups. The crowds who listened must have been composed of men and women, children and young people, country folk and the sophisticates from the city. One suspects that, for example, the story of the Good Samaritan was told with very much more colour, detail and action than the rather bald version that we have in Luke's Gospel. No good storyteller would leave such a wonderful story with so little detail and colour. It would have been understood differently by the different elements of the crowd. The children would have enjoyed the simple storyline, the adults would have been shocked by the thought of a 'good' Samaritan, and the religious leaders would have been furious with Jesus for his attack upon their own kind.

In the same way a story told at all-age events will be appreciated at different levels. If, for example, you tell a fanciful story about Napoleon the earwig that lives in a cardboard box at the back of the church, the children will enjoy the storyline and perhaps little else, while the adults will realise that the story was really about envy and it may make them question their own values.

Everyone, even the youngster who has just come home from playschool, can tell a story, and so much of our conversation revolves around story in one shape or other. Yet the art of being a good storyteller does not belong to everyone.

In this our computer age, with its analytical thinking,

the art of storytelling is undergoing a revival. The reason
for this and all the theory and practice of storytelling for
the Christian can be found in William J. Bausch's highly
recommended book, *Storytelling: Imagination and Faith*
(details in Appendix).

Everyone can develop storytelling skills. The secrets are:

1. to know the story well, so that it flows;
2. to stand or sit in a commanding position, so that the
   audience can see every movement;
3. to use the whole body in the telling, hands and arms,
   gestures and facial expressions;
4. to use simple 'props' as visual aids to illustrate the
   storyline;
5. to use silence, where it fits, for effect;
6. to involve the audience in the telling as much as
   possible;
7. to have a clear and tidy ending.

A very valuable all-age learning event could explore the
use of storytelling by Jesus; or the use of parables today;
or how to become a better Christian storyteller.

USING THE INGREDIENTS

It would be unthinkable to have a Christian act of worship
without the use, in some form or other, of Holy Scripture.

Christian boys and girls who are educated in our secondary schools alongside Jewish young people of the Orthodox
tradition learn some interesting lessons. When the Jewish
young person does his RE homework he writes 'G-d' for
God. When the day of Yom Kippur comes round the Christ-

ians learn that the Jewish community are fasting from all food for twenty-four hours for their sins. The Jewish children command respect because of their own respect for God's name and the dignified practice of their Faith.

In our increasing multi-cultured schools, Moslem pupils also win respect for refusing to eat or drink from sunrise to sunset during the whole month of Ramadan. With the respect that both these world faiths give to their sacred writings – you have to wash your hands before you may touch the Q'uran – such pupils must be amazed at the total lack of respect that Christian pupils accord the Bible.

The first ingredient in any all-age Christian act of worship must be the dignified use of the Bible. The public reading of the Word of God should be accompanied by some acts or easily understood signs that show that we do love, honour and respect Holy Scripture.

This central feature of the liturgy of the Word can be illustrated or given dramatic impact by the use of drama, movement, dance or puppets, but never in such a way as to trivialise or detact from the dignity that must always be accorded to God's Word. In a desire to make the Scriptures clear and understandable we must not make them cheap. It is imperative that our children and young people grow up to respect them.

If there are to be individual copies of the Bible in the church pews – although this would seem unnecessary if the Word of God is publically read and proclaimed well – the books should be in good condition.

Music is the next ingredient which, as we have seen, should support or at least not distract from the theme of the act of worship. Much experimentation can take place, not only in the styles of music, but the instruments used, the best place for the musicians to be, etc. The community will almost certainly have more musicians than have volunteered and come forward. A talent inventory might uncover much that could be used to enrich the community's worship.

The problem with a talent inventory in a church community is not how to conduct it but how best to use what it reveals. Such an inventory can be conducted in several ways. It can be a section in a wider review of details such as addresses and contacts, or a separate 'What can you offer your church?' questionnaire. In addition to asking 'Do you play an instrument?' and 'Have you artistic skills?', it could include questions about willingness to visit the sick or join a drivers' list for lifts for elderly folk who find transport difficult.

Too often inventories are taken and then never followed up and used properly. How to make best use of the information should be discussed and structures arranged before the inventory is conducted. Otherwise expectations are raised in the community which are never realised.

3

CELEBRATING THE CHRISTIAN YEAR

THE CHRISTIAN YEAR

It is a puzzle to many children and young people that we celebrate the birth of Jesus and then less than four months later we are talking about his death on the cross. While the Christian year helps us to enter more deeply into the mystery of Christ's life, death and resurrection, it is not helpful to suggest that the year is tied to or follows the order of his life, which it clearly does not.

It is more understandable for ordinary people if we approach the mystery of Christ through his twin commandments: 'love God' and 'love your neighbour'. The simplest and most helpful description of God in the New Testament is in the first letter of John, 'God is love' (4:16). It is from our appreciation of God's love for us and our developing love for him, that our faith, hope and love are nourished.

One way to understand and use the Christian year is to see it in terms of love, inspired by the simple phrase, 'love came down at Christmas', and prompted by the text, 'God so loved the world that he gave his son' (John 3:16):

The Coming of Love	–	Advent
The Showing of Love	–	Christmas and Epiphany

The Offering of Love   – Lent and Holy Week
The Triumph of Love   – Easter
The Giving of Love   – Pentecost
The Living of Love   – Time after Pentecost

Advent: The Coming of Love

This preparation period of the Christian year, called 'the Coming', is well named for Advent covers not one but three 'comings' of Christ:

1. The coming of 'Love' as a baby – the first coming of Jesus as a member of the human family.
2. The coming of 'Love' as a preacher – the second coming of Jesus at the age of thirty as a rabbi.
3. The coming of 'Love' as the judge – the final coming of Christ at the end of time as our judge and king.

In the four weeks of Advent these three 'comings' of Jesus are recalled. In worship where very young children are involved it might prove confusing if more than the first coming is concentrated on. However older children need not be confused, if there is clear and careful explanation. Few older parishioners will have realised that Advent has these three threads to it, and their observance of the season might be freshened and become more satisfying with the realisation.

Just as in family life, so in the family life of the community, much is learnt in an accumulative way by constant repetition. The Christian year, like the seasons, comes round and round again. We do not need to be anxious about doing, learning and understanding everything at once.

Christmas and Epiphany:
The Showing of Love

The birth of a first baby is an exciting time in a family. With understandable pride the parents show off the sign of their love for one another to family, friends and neighbours, and church communities should try never to miss the opportunity to be part of this loving celebration. The genuine joy and expressions of love and support from everyone around the couple make the occasion unique in all human experience.

Christmas is surely the most popular of the Christian festivals because deep down, beyond all the commercialism it is the celebration of such a love. At the divine level God shows his love by the gift of his Son. At the human level a young couple, Mary and Joseph, have a first baby and, having no family close by, show the child off, first to the shepherds and later to the Magi. Setting aside here any questions of literary criticism, Luke and Matthew, in their quite different versions of the Nativity story, point to the future role of the baby through these 'showings'. For the future Messiah will be the Good Shepherd as well as Lord of all nations and King of kings.

Christmas is a birthday celebration, not of a dead hero but of a living Lord. There would be no Christmas festival if there were no triumphant resurrection. It is the risen Lord we celebrate with at Christmas. So the festival is less about an historical event (so it is unimportant that we do not know for sure the day or even the year), and more about celebrating Christ's continuing presence with us.

Lent and Holy Week: The Offering of Love

'Canoe leader risks life to keep group together.'
'Wife throws herself in front of husband as terrorist fires.'

From time to time our daily newspapers carry stories of heroic self-sacrifice, when the natural impulse for self-preservation is courageously set aside. Such generous action does not come naturally, for all humans are born with a necessary strong self-love. With the passing of the years this has to be broadened out, channelled and developed, so that while retaining a healthy self-love (to take proper care of oneself) ingrowing love is turned out to include others.

The learning goes on all through life, the really mature person being the one who is most unselfish, with the greatest love and consideration for others. Jesus summed it up when he said, 'Greater love has no one than this, that he lay down his life for his friends' (John 15:13).

For most Christians the effort to live unselfishly is a daily struggle. Self-discipline is called for, and Lent is the season which encourages us to concentrate on this in preparation for Easter, the celebration of Christ's heroic self-sacrifice.

So Lent is

– a time for a change of heart, for a closer look at the way our lives are lived.
– a time for concern for others, caring by personal action or gifts to charity.
– a time for prayer that costs, in terms of time and effort.

All three strike at personal selfishness and the roots of sin. A closer look at our lives will reveal areas that need dealing with; concern for others encourages us to put others before our own self-interest; and an effort to set time aside for prayer helps us to put God first and receive help to live the Christian life. Only Easter, when the Lord offered himself for us, makes sense of Lent. We cannot spiritually go down into the grave with Christ on Good Friday and rise up to a new life with him on Easter Day, if we have not made some preparation beforehand. 'If we die with him, we will also live with him' (2 Timothy 2:11).

Easter: The Triumph of Love

The Israelites were so triumphant, after they had passed safely out of slavery in Egypt and through the Red Sea, that they burst into song (Exodus 15:1–18): 'In your unfailing love you will lead the people you have redeemed' (v. 13).

That triumph of God's love has been celebrated by the Jewish People from that day to this in the annual festival of Pesah or Passover. It recalls how blood shed and placed on the door frame protected the people of Israel when the firstborn of the Egyptians died, the final blow that persuaded Pharaoh to let the people go.

Was it just providential or by the deliberate planning of Christ that his arrest, death and resurrection took place at Pesah? Of all the days in the year none were more appropriate and significant. From the very earliest days of Christianity, even before Christ's followers were called 'Christians', the vital link and connection of 'the Lamb of God's' sacrificial death and triumphant resurrection with the events of Exodus 11–20 were appreciated.

Once the Christian appreciates the significance of the triumph of God's love at the first passover, in Egypt, and the triumph of God's love in the 'passover' of Christ, then the realisation dawns that the resurrection theme is at the very centre of each individual's life.

It is not just the seasons that see the 'death' and 'rebirth' of nature, nor each day that 'dies' at dusk and 'rises afresh' at dawn. Daily each Christian is tempted, falls and 'rises' to follow Christ anew.

How many times in every normal person's life is there a losing and a finding; a crisis and a recovery; a loss of employment and a new opening; a breakdown in friendship and a new love; an illness and a restoration to good health; a death in the family and a birth? And for the faithful Christian 'all things work together for good' and for the final triumph of love.

Pentecost: The Giving of Love

In secondary education these days, pupils are encouraged to learn at least two foreign languages. They will also learn other 'languages'. There is, for example, computer 'language', there is 'body language', and when they start to drive they will have to master the language of the Highway Code.

According to Genesis God intended that the unity of the human race should be assured through the use of just one language. Human pride brought confusion, as the Tower of Babel story explains (Genesis 11:1–9), and when 'the Lord confused the language of the whole world' disunity reigned.

Lovers speak the same language, in more than one sense, and often have their own 'language'. Love shares knowledge. God so loved the world that he spoke his Word in human terms (Christmas). The Word of God, or the Son, so loved God the Father that he gave total obedience and the sacrifice of his whole self (Easter).

Because of his nature God communicates, as we do, through signs, and Pentecost is rich in God's sign language. 'Suddenly a sound like the blowing of a violent wind came from heaven and filled the whole house ... they saw what seemed to be tongues of fire that separated and came to rest on each of them' (Acts 2:2–3).

The fire of God's love enters the lives of the Apostles and they are transformed. The 'tongues' of Pentecost heal and unite, where the 'tongues' of Babel had sown division and disunity.

The 'language' of love is a gift; lovers always want to give to one another. In the parable of the last judgment in Matthew 25:31–46, the separation of sheep from goats, it is those who are the 'givers' who are rewarded, while the takers are banished to eternal punishment. Eternal life is for those who have shown their love for Christ by serving their neighbours, according to the model given them by the Suffering Servant at the Last Supper meal (John 13:1–16). This love is the gift of the Spirit of Love bestowed at Pentecost.

Time After Pentecost: The Living of Love

It is one thing to receive a gift, quite another to appreciate and use it. The gift of God's love is offered to all and particularly to those who, following Christ, have shown some desire to live by his way. Indeed those first followers who lived by the gift of the Spirit were called 'the people of the way' (Acts 9:2 and 24:14). However only a small number respond to the gift and that response varies from person to person.

The Parable of the Sower comes to mind, where the seed is the gift of God's Spirit of Love. Some seed fell along the path, where it was trampled on. Some fell on rock, where it withered away. Some fell among thorns and it was choked by them. And some fell on good soil, yielding a crop.

The gift is the same, the response is individual. God never forces anyone.

The traditional colour used for church vestments at this time of the year is green, the colour of growth. The growth looked for is not in church attendance or 'churchy' activities but in personal development, in the yield of a good crop.

Living a life of love in a family setting is one of constant service, and it is often an uphill struggle to respond generously. There is the endless round of clearing up after children, sorting out their squabbles, keeping up with the boring round of washing, ironing, cooking. No other way of life offers so much aggravation and temptation to quit, nor such an opportunity to grow in patience, in love and maturity. The living of love in the family is the God-given way for most Christians to grow.

Much the same can be said of those who care for a physically or mentally handicapped person, an aging and bedridden relative, or a terminally ill patient. It is a living out of the Easter theme, of dying to oneself in the service of others. The badge of the true Christian is the apron, the apron of the Suffering Servant.

PRACTICAL POINTERS

The loneliness of the person who lives alone can be crucifying too, especially in our society where it can be accentuated by the fear of going out after dark. The local church

family needs to be aware of such people and help them to
grow by drawing them too into an 'apron' Christianity.
(Growth does not stop because people are in their eighties
or house-bound.) There are always interests and tasks available to such members of the community, if there is a
willingness to serve, though their willingness may need
nurturing by confidence-building. The tasks can be as
simple as making tea or coffee for the harassed helpers at
the church mother and toddler group, or reading to the
children of such a group. It could be baby-sitting so that a
young couple can go out and have a little time to themselves; sitting with a bedridden church member; helping
with a Christian Aid coffee morning etc. If practical action
is difficult, there is still the valuable work of prayer. Our
daily papers and the community's sick list will provide
plenty of reasons to pray.

The work of the Spirit is growth, in unity, love, joy and
peace. The church community grows through mutual
service and everyone of whatever age or situation can
follow the example of Christ the Servant, if they appreciate
and use the gifts of the Holy Spirit.

A Note on Charismatic Gifts

All Christians receive charismatic gifts, and all Christians
are charismatics. For 'No one can say, Jesus is Lord, except
by the Holy Spirit' (1 Corinthians 12:3). No genuine gift
of the Holy Spirit will ever divide or estrange others, nor
will it breed pride, for that is the way of Babel, not the way
of Pentecost.

Charismatic gifts are not for the individual and personal
use of a Christian. Christianity is a community faith, as we

saw earlier, so the gifts of the Spirit are for the upbuilding of the Christian as a member of the community. Each gift is for sharing and for the development of the community. 'The manifestation of the Spirit is for the common good' (1 Corinthians 12:7).

The most important of all the gifts is that which is seen clearly in the life of Jesus himself, the humble, loving service of others. 'And now I will show you the most excellent way...' (1 Corinthians 12:31)

Harvest

In modern urban life the Christian link with the soil and with gathering in the harvest has become tenuous. Most of us are more familiar with stacks of canned food, often from the tropics. Yet the Harvest Festival can still play an important liturgical role, not only in expressing gratitude to our Creator Father for all his goodness and care of us, but also as a celebration of the gathering in of a spiritual harvest, along the lines that we have been exploring.

All Saints

The festival of All Saints , which ends the Christian year, is easily linked with the harvest of the fruits of the Spirit, in those members of our local community whose lives have been an admirable example.

All Saints' tide provides the opportunity to turn away from the ordinary time of the Church Year in an autumn month that has its own secular echoes of death and remembering. Sanctity is – in spite of everything – accessible to people, not as a nice idea but as a reality pumped into the blood-stream of the human race by God's action in the lives of his saints. The dark side of that confident rejoicing in our fellowship with the saints is the Church mourning her departed and commending them in faith and trust to God. This commemoration is a proper corrective to the rather forced jollity which is sometimes substituted for a sober confidence in the power of God alone to bring life out of death, light out of darkness. While we rejoice in the heroic example of the saints, we feel the loss of those we know and love, and many people are helped by holding together these two commemorations.

THE PROMISE OF HIS GLORY

IDEAS FOR ALL-AGE SERVICES BASED ON THE CHRISTIAN YEAR

This section offers guidelines for complete all-age events based on the Christian year. Teams who are exploring all-age worship for the first time may find them useful guides. Others may find some ideas, insights or readings to add to their own store of experience.

Advent

BACKGROUND NOTES

The word 'Advent' is derived from the Latin for 'coming' or 'arrival'. The season was developed in the Western Church as a preparation for the Nativity, in imitation of

Lent, which is much earlier in origin. Church councils held in Gaul in the sixth century refer to Advent as a period of six weeks before Christmas, with fasting on each Monday, Wednesday and Friday. In other countries five weeks was the norm. However by the eighth century, throughout Europe, Advent had become a four-week season.

BIBLICAL NOTES

From a biblical perspective the words 'coming' and 'Messiah' are inter-connected. The expected coming of the Messiah is what is celebrated throughout Advent and Christmas. Through the dark days of the Exile in Babylon and the oppression of Greek and Roman occupation, the Jewish People longed for a 'Son of David' to come. So Isaiah could prophesy: 'The people walking in darkness have seen a great light; on those living in the land of the shadow of death a light has dawned' (Isaiah 9:2).

VISUAL/DECORATION

Advent is a time of preparation for the joy and excitement of Christmas, a quiet 'low' period before the 'high' of the festive season. So it is traditional not to have flower arrangements during Advent. In fact it is an ideal time to get a work party together to give the church a thorough clean and tidy up. The stark simplicity of Advent is an important reminder of its role.

Advent wreaths have become widely used in recent years. Many churches place a large evergreen wreath, with four red candles (some add a white one in the centre, as a Christmas candle) on a table clearly to view near the altar. During the introductory rites a child is invited to come forward and light the candle for that Sunday.

JESSE TREE

Not so common is the custom of the Jesse Tree, which dates from the Middle Ages. A branch of a large bush or a small tree is stripped of its leaves, painted silver, and set in a bucket of sand. On the branches the children hang cut-out figures representing people and events in the Old Testament that prepared the way for the coming of Jesus. For example, creation can be symbolised by a cut-out sun and moon, the fall of Adam and Eve by an apple, Noah and family by a cardboard ark, Isaac by a bundle of sticks, Jacob by a ladder, King David by a harp, and so on.

EXPLORING THE THEME

The key features of Advent are the Coming of the Messiah and the Kingdom that he preached; the watching and waiting; the expectant longing, in a spirit of penitence, for the fulfilment of the promise made to the people of the old covenant.

Modern Christians, affected by non-Christian popular culture, may start celebrating the Nativity, with Christmas trees and decorations long before 25th December. But in the Church year the celebrating begins on the 25th and extends to 6th January.

MUSIC

Christmas carols have little place in Advent, so try to avoid popular pressure to use them before 24th December. This will not be easy, and resistance to their use should always be accompanied by an explanation. Simply put, you cannot expectantly wait for the arrival of something and simultaneously sing in celebration of its arrival!

Advent music should be chosen to reflect the theme.

The following are suitable choices. (The numbers refer to *Mission Praise*, and *Junior Praise*)

Come, thou long-expected Jesus (102, 335)
Darkness like a shroud (110, 658)
El-Shaddai (119, 341)
Faithful vigil ended (125, 660)
Hark, the glad sound (210, 385)
How lovely on the mountains (249, 79)
When He comes (752, 625)

READINGS

In the ASB and the Roman Lectionary the emphasis in the readings for the first two Sundays of Advent is on the coming of Christ as judge. There is a shift to his coming as a child and as a preacher on the last two Sundays.

If you plan to cover all three 'comings' in one Advent Service (are not three necessary?), the following outline could be used:

'Your God is coming' (Isaiah 35:1-6, 10) – the coming of the Messiah as preacher.

'Be Patient' (James 5:7-10) – his coming as Judge.

'She will give birth to a son' (Matthew 1:18-25) – the coming of the Incarnate Word.

INTRODUCTION

Four volunteers are needed to stand before the people in a line to take the parts below (or similar ones). In addition four children (two for each poster) hold two five-foot lengths of wallpaper with the words clearly printed, COMING and HOPE. These can be held on either side of the four volunteers so that people can see them clearly. The four speakers say:

'I am an expectant mother. The birth of my baby is coming ... I hope for a healthy baby.'

'I am a school boy. The Christmas holidays are coming ... I hope for lots of Christmas presents.'

'I am a pensioner. My family are coming to see me at Christmas ... I hope to find them all well and happy.'

'I am a driver/florist/sceretary. My retirement is coming soon ... I am hoping for time to expand my interests.'

The minister or leader now says: 'The key words of each of our friends' statements are COMING and HOPE, and these are the key words for the whole of Advent, and our service today.'

The service proceeds with the opening hymn or call to worship.

Children's address

The minister or leader can hide a box of sweets near to where he or she is to speak. A large card, nicely decorated, with the word CHRISTMAS clearly printed on it needs to be propped up in a position where the leader can walk past it and have space before and after the card. The children's address can go along these lines:

In a few minutes I am going to invite all of you children to come up here and I will give you something. Now, you are very interested; you want to know what it is you will receive; you are hoping for something good; there is an air of expectancy; you are beginning to think, how long have we got to wait?

That is what it was like for the Jewish people before the birth of Jesus, the Messiah. They believed that God would send them a good leader. They were waiting in hope.

(Leader walks to the far side of the large card.) In front of me is the word CHRISTMAS. It's like that now; Christmas lies ahead of us, just a few more weeks to go. If I walk slowly towards this word, CHRISTMAS, that is like the passing of time. Now I have arrived at the card and, before I know it, I'm past. Christmas is behind me. Now I have to look back to it.

That is what happens every year; Christmas seems a long time coming and then it is all over. (You are still waiting and hoping for what I have hidden for you.) The Jewish people waited for a long time for Jesus to be born, as the Christ; and because he was not quite what they had expected, many of them did not accept God's gift.

You are all anxious to know what it is that I have for you; you must wait patiently. That is what the Jewish people had to do as they waited for the Messiah to be born; they had to be patient.

That is the lesson of Advent; we have to learn patience. God will always answer our prayers, but not necessarily in the way we expect, and sometimes he makes us wait quite a long time for an answer. But it will come.

(Speaker returns to starting point and produces the box of sweets.) Now the time has come. Come up two or three at a time and help yourselves to a sweet.

Advent Wreath

After the Gospel reading the first (or next) candle may be lit. (See *The Promise of His Glory*, p. 137, for an accompanying prayer.)

Adults' address

Three of the previous four volunteers are needed again: the expectant mother, the school child and the pensioner. (Take care to balance the genders.) They are asked to stand near the speaker, in full view. The card used for the children is replaced with one which has the words: Baby, Teacher, Judge. The leader says:

We have already learnt that the season of Advent is about the words COMING and HOPE. You heard how the children were told that another important word is PATIENCE. How do these three words link with our three volunteers standing here, and with Advent itself? Let's all go and stand beside the card which has the words, Baby, Teacher, and Judge. (Group stands to left of the card, as seen by the congregation.)

There are three 'comings' of Christ, as baby, as teacher and, in the future, as judge. Our expectant mother here is waiting patiently for the coming of her baby, and with her we all hope it will be strong and healthy when it is born. (The woman crosses to the other side of the card.) Jesus has already come as a baby.

When we see our school girl (boy) standing here we see the uniform and we are reminded of our local school and its teachers. (Name of child) has to patiently learn at school and hopes that the teachers will give a proper, balanced education. (Child crosses to the other side of the card.) Jesus has already come as a teacher.

Our pensioner here is grateful for the many life experiences he/she has had and is aware of successes and failures in the past. Aware too that at some point in the future Christ will pass a judgment on them. But that has not yet come; Christ has still to come as judge for each one of us. (Speaker returns to original point, leaving the expectant mother and the child on the left of the card and the pensioner still standing on the left.)

The season of Advent is given to us to remember and think about these three 'comings' of Christ. So the readings of Advent speak of John the Baptist who prepared the people for the arrival of Jesus as a teacher; and there are readings too to remind us that Christ will judge each of us, at the end of our own lives and at the end of the world. So Advent is not just about preparing for the birth of the special baby on 25th December, as the Advent calendars would have us believe.

PRAYERS OF INTERCESSION

These can be led by the four volunteers.

Expectant mother:
Caring Creator and Father,
you have made all things and care
for the tiniest of your creatures.
As we prepare for the birthday
of your Son as a tiny child,
we ask your blessing on all women
who are expecting a child,
the work of your creation.
        Prepare us, O Lord.
Response: Make us ready for Christ's coming.

Schoolchild:
Father of all knowledge and wisdom,
you desire all people to grow
in understanding and develop
to their fullest potential.
As we prepare for the birthday
of your Son, who became the world's
greatest and most important teacher,
we ask your blessing on all who teach
and learn in our local schools.
        Prepare us, O Lord.
Response: Make us ready for Christ's coming.

Pensioner:
Ageless God and Father,
you live a timeless existence
and never grow old.
As we prepare for the birthday
of your son, who shared all the
joys and anxieties that we experience,
we ask your blessing on those who
are worried about aging, living alone
and their health.
Prepare us, O Lord.
Response: Make us ready for Christ's coming.

A person nearing retirement:
Generous Lord and Father,
you loved the world so much
that you gave us your Son.
As we prepare for the birthday
of your Son, who took the model
of the Suffering Servant,
we ask your blessing on all those
who serve the community.
Prepare us, O Lord.
Response: Make us ready for Christ's coming.

Naturally other intercessory prayers may be added.

PARTING SCRIPTS

Reproduce the following twelve texts, cut them into individual little scripts and roll them tightly, so that each one comes out as a tiny scroll. Produce enough for every person at the service to have one, then pack them, mixed up, like little cylinders in two or three boxes. Arrange for two or three of the volunteers to stand at the church door as the

people leave. Before the final blessing, the minister should
encourage all to take a 'thought' for Advent as they leave.

Let us live
faithfully, justly, peacefully,
in this world,
awaiting the blessed hope
and advent of the glory
of the great God.

We wait for your loving
kindness, O God,
to be revealed to us.

O Lord of hosts, restore us,
if your face shine upon us,
then we shall be safe.

The people who walked
in darkness,
shall see a great light.

Withhold your wrath
from us, O Lord,
and remember no more
our evil doing.

Lord, let me hear the call
of your prophet, John,
that I may truly repent
and prepare.

Let what is crooked in me
become straight,
let what is rough become
    smooth,
and what is empty be filled.

May God the Father,
who loved the world so much
    that he gave his Son,
give you grace to prepare
for everlasting life.

May God himself,
the God of everlasting
   peace,
make you perfect and
   holy
for the coming of his Son,
Jesus Christ.

Lord Jesus, the prophets said
you would bring peace.
Give peace to our troubled
   hearts,
this Christmastide,
and always.

Lord Jesus,
   John told the people
to prepare,
   for you were very near.
As Christmas approaches
help me to be ready
to welcome your
coming.

When you come,
   as judge,
Lord Jesus,
May you find me
ready and prepared.

Christmas

BACKGROUND NOTE

It is at Rome in the early fourth century that we find the first
evidence of Christmas being celebrated by the Christian

community. In AD 274 the Emperor Aurelian introduced in the imperial capital the Festival of the Invincible Sun (Natalis Solis Invicti) on 25th December. At some point before AD 336 (the first recorded date of Christmas) the Church, having no certain date of Christ's birth, must have taken this date to commemorate the Incarnation, the birth of the Sun of Righteousness.

BIBLICAL NOTE

The nativity stories occur in only two places in the New Testament, the first two chapters of both Matthew and Luke. These stories stand in isolation and arise from traditions different from those found elsewhere in the four Gospels. There are tensions between the two versions.

Modern Christians need to read reflectively what the text actually says, as distinct from what they think it says. For example the visitors from the East are 'Magi', astrologers, not 'kings' (Matthew 2:1). It does not say there were three; three gifts can be brought by four people or ten people. They did not find a baby in a stable, the child was probably about eighteen months old (see v. 16), and the family were dwelling in a house, 'on coming to the house' (v. 11).

The key text which sums up the message of Christmas is from John's Gospel, 'The Word became flesh and made his dwelling among us' (John 1:14). Essentially Christmas is not the celebration of a past historical event but of the wondrous belief that the Son of God became one of us and, as the risen Christ, is ever-present with us.

VISUAL/DECORATION

Most churches have their own customs, but it is good to question these, from time to time, to bring freshness, and to ensure that they are achieving their aim. Decoration can be for decoration's sake (good in itself), or it can be used to teach at the same time. This, of course, was the purpose of the old pre-Reformation wall paintings in parish churches.

Another challenge is to involve more than a small group (clique?) in the work of decoration. It is possible to share out the window sills, the pillars, etc, among the church groups, not forgetting the children and young people. All-age decoration, in other words. The Guides, Scouts, Brownies etc can be allotted a portion of the church, along with the women's groups (and men's?). The regular decorators can take care of the big Christmas tree or the crib, if there is one.

Crib decorators should be discouraged from putting the kings or wise men in or near the crib. According to Matthew's Gospel these visitors did not arrive at Christmas but some time later. These figures should therefore only be added on the feast of the Epiphany, 6th January. This will give an added focus for that great festival, which is otherwise easily very overshadowed. A visual for the Epiphany is given later.

The decorating working parties would find it helpful and encouraging if they are given themes for their designs, eg, Light of the World, Holy Family, Prince of Peace, Dwelt among us, Glory to God.

INTRODUCTION

As soon as all are gathered, before the commencement of the service proper, a minister stands before the congregation with a basket of fresh holly leaves (already stripped from the branch). He or she invites two people from each bench, or each family, the youngest and eldest, to come forward. As they approach the minister places a holly leaf carefully in the open palm of the hand, with the words, 'Keep a generous open hand, like God.' They return to their places. The minister addresses the people, along these lines:

This is a joyous day, a happy occasion, but it is not without its reminder of the painful side of life. The Christians of the Middle Ages appreciated that the birth of the Son of God was not without pain and inconvenience. They used the holly bush, with its evergreen leaves and prickly thorns, as a symbol. The evergreen reminds us of the ever-present risen Christ who helps us to grow as Christians. The sharp prickles remind us of the crown of thorns of Jesus, before he died for us. They also remind us that our lives have 'prickly' parts to them.

The holly leaves were given out with the words, 'Keep a generous open hand, like God,' to remind us today of God's openhanded generosity – he so loved the world that he gave his son. If you close your hand, if you are tightfisted with others, there will be pain, not happiness.

Now sing together the carol 'The Holly and the Ivy'. (This can be the opening hymn of the service.)

EXPLORING THE THEME

The Christmas celebration is about the wondrous mystery of the Incarnation. It is not so much the birth of the historical Jesus that we seek to recall, but the meaning for us now of the Word made flesh and the presence with us of the Risen Christ of Faith. It is possible for modern Christians to be too content with looking back two thousand years to a baby in a manger and to fail to understand the deeper significance of the festival.

MUSIC

This is not the time for new hymns and experimentation. There will be people in the congregation who do not attend regularly and they should not feel excluded by the choice of music. Many carols, ancient and modern, are popular and suitable.

READINGS

These are well known and prescribed by tradition. If this service is taking the place of a family service on Christmas morning then any reading(s) preceding the following drama should be kept very short.

Select four 'actors' to take the parts in the following short dramatic presentation, rehearse and provide them with costumes.

Before the service begins they are in the church, welcoming the congregation (answering no questions about their role in the service), giving out hymn books, etc.

Before the Gospel reading, the 'actors' come to the front and face the congregation to present 'The No-Good Shepherd Boy'. This is followed by the Gospel reading, Luke chapter 2, verses 4–16.

The No-Good Shepherd Boy

Scene:	In a market area of Jerusalem, near the Sheep Gate.
Time:	Early evening on 24th December, 6BC.
Present:	A scruffy-looking shepherd, a young lad.
	A richly adorned woman, middle-aged.
	A priest, elderly.
	A modestly dressed woman, elderly.

Shepherd: I've come into the city to buy some food for our group; it's likely to be cold out in the fields tonight. We spend all our time with the sheep. We can't get to the synagogue on the Sabbath. And everyone else looks down on us because we can't keep all the purity laws.

Rich woman: I'm the wife of a very rich Sadducee. My husband owns several shops and has a prosperous trading company. Of course he attends the local synagogue and we bought it a new scroll only last week. What is this scruffy shepherd doing here?

Priest: I am one of the chief priests. I've just come from working in the Temple all day, we offered thirty-seven sacrifices today. The temple is my life. I keep every one of the Jewish laws and I know God is pleased with me. What is that irreligious shepherd doing here? It's about time they were banned from coming into the Holy City.

Elderly woman: My husband is the oldest serving member of the Sanhedrin, the Council. He's a highly respected rabbi and pharisee, well-known for the long religious fasts he keeps. We have a lovely country house out at Bethlehem and an apartment here in the city. My husband would soon send this filthy shepherd boy packing.

Shepherd (aside to congregation:): You see, these respectable folk have no time for the likes of me.

Rich woman: Excuse me, but I must be off. My husband

	and I are invited to a smart party at the High Priest's house this evening.
Priest:	I beg your pardon, but I must go too. The priests have a meeting this evening to discuss the new rota of services at the Temple.
Elderly woman:	Excuse me but I must hurry home. My husband expects me home for the evening family prayers at dusk.
Shepherd:	You see how nice respectable people look down on us shepherds. No parties for us, nothing exciting ever happens in our lives, it's so boring looking after sheep.

MUSIC

The carol 'While shepherds watch' or 'Glory to God' can come immediately before or after the Gospel reading.

If the church has an orchestral group some light pieces can be played softly in the background during the readings. If there is no such group, Christmas is a fine opportunity to get together a few young flutists, guitarists, etc, to provide a simple background or accompaniment. (There is no need to be too adventurous to begin with.)

ADDRESS

The theme of today is the dignity of the individual human person, arising from the belief that God's Son, the Word, became a human person. The Son of God became man so that mankind could become sons of God. The divine seal was placed upon human dignity the moment the Word was born in the Bethlehem stable.

Did you get the point of 'The No-Good Shepherd Boy'? Bethlehem is within walking distance of Jerusalem, and at the time of Christ's birth there were many very religious people, many very wealthy people. There was the High Priest and members of his Council; the rich merchants of the Sadducee families and members of the supreme council, the Sanhedrin. But not one of those was invited to the birth of the Messiah. When the long-awaited historic moment arrived, the birth of the promised Messiah, no religious or community leader was invited; only the looked-down-on, marginalised shepherds. What a message for us.

Where would Christ be born today? Who would be invited? Perhaps it would be among the homeless on London's streets; in the doorway of Boots, along the Strand. Who would be invited? Would the angel call at Buckingham Palace and leave an invitation there, or at Lambeth Palace for the Archbishop of Canterbury? According to Luke's Gospel, no. Who are the modern equivalent to the shepherds? Who do we respectable, religious and fairly well-off people look down on?

God so loved the world – the poor, the disabled, the illiterate – that he gave his Son. Christmas is about human dignity. God does not judge people by what they possess, or the education they have received, or their career prospects. He does not 'see' colour or age or sex; God sees the loving heart. On this gift-giving day make a gift to God before you leave this church today – the genuine gift of your heart. Let us now sing the first and last verses of 'In the bleak mid-winter'. Apply the symbolism of the first verse, not to the weather, but to the bleak materialistic world in which we live, where so many people's hearts are closed to those in need, are prejudiced against others, and are as 'hard as iron' in their business dealings.

Epiphany

BACKGROUND NOTE

The word Epiphany comes from the Greek for 'manifestation'. The feast day has a long and complex history. At first, in the Eastern Church from the third century, the manifestation referred to the revelation of God to the world in Jesus Christ. By the fourth century it was commemorating the birth of Jesus and his baptism. When the Western Church established the 25th December as the Festival of the Lord's birth, the 6th January became the manifestation of the Child Jesus to the Magi. It is still kept as the festival of the Lord's baptism in the Eastern Church.

BIBLICAL NOTE

The Scripture text (Matthew 2:1–18) is overlaid with tradition. In the planning meeting it would be advisable to read the text and discuss it together. It is the symbolism of the gifts which is important, pointing to the type of Messiah Jesus will be, not the number of the visitors or their traditional names. Matthew is keen to convince his Jewish readers that this very special child really does fulfil the Old Testament prophecies.

VISUAL/DECORATION

The symbolism of the three gifts is important and rather than emphasise the gift-bringers (the Magi), who have their own symbolic purpose, the decoration can focus on the gold, incense and myrrh. However, if the church uses a Christmas crib the figures of the Magi can 'journey' to the stable, beginning the first Sunday after Christmas. They can start just inside the church, preferably on a table or some raised area, and can be moved every day to arrive on 6th, then be placed in the crib at the commencement of that day's service.

There could be three flower arrangements, one for each gift, with the symbolism of each explored – regal colours with a touch of the oriental; for the incense, blue and silver; and for the myrrh, purple and magenta. Or one large arrangement could include all these colours.

Exploring the Theme

The visitors to the child Jesus were not Jews, yet their story is only recorded in the Gospel written by a Jew, Matthew, for Jewish readers. So the 'showing' of Christ to the Gentiles must be significant. The gifts relate to the future role of the child as Messiah. For the Gentiles (and the Jews) he will be a king (gold), a priest (frankincense), and a suffering servant (myrrh), just as the prophets had foretold.

Music

Suitable music could include the following (numbers from *Mission Praise*):

As with gladness men of old (39)
In Christ there is no east or west (329)
Jesus shall reign (379)
Let all the world in every corner sing (404)
We three kings (740)

Readings

Isaiah 49:1–6: 'I will make you a light to the Gentiles.' The young girl who led in the ministers, stands beside (a little behind) the reader during this reading.

Or Isaiah 60:1–6: 'Nations will come to your light, and

kings to the brightness of your dawn.' If there has been the opportunity to work with the children, these words (or the previous text) can appear on a decorated card and be held up beside the star.

Ephesians 3:1–12 or 3:2–3a, 5–6: 'The Gentiles are heirs together with Israel, members together of one body, sharers in the promise of Christ Jesus.'

Matthew 2:1–12: This reading is ideally suited for either a dramatised reading in parts, or acting out with actors' own parts and words, but well prepared and rehearsed. (See *The Dramatised Bible.*) It is vital that the parts are shared out with all ages in mind. The wise 'men' do not have to be adult males and there can be a deliberate decision to have five or six visitors; this can be explained in the sermon.

INTRODUCTION

The choir and the ministers could be led in, today, by a young girl (not vested) who carries a large silver star on a stick or pole. (The star can be simply made of card, covered with kitchen foil, mounted on a spare broom handle.)

If appropriate, when all are gathered, the Magi crib figures can be ceremonially placed in the crib by people of different ages. The figures could be brought in as part of the entry procession, led by the star-bearer and to the accompaniment of the hymn, 'We three kings'.

CHILDREN'S ADDRESS

The star-bearer comes to stand beside the speaker. A boy goes to the crib and brings the 'baby', then stands beside the bearer of the star. The address is along these lines.

Did anyone here get a bike for Christmas? Did you go

out and ride it on Christmas Day? Did you show it to your friends? (More of the like.) When we have a lovely gift we like to show it to our friends. We want people to admire it.

You see our star, here. The star showed the Wise Men where the baby Jesus was. When the Magi arrived at the house, not the stable, where Mary and Joseph were, Mary showed Jesus to the visitors from the East. That is why this day is called the 'Epiphany', because the word means, 'the Showing'. Jesus was God's very special gift. He was born a Jewish baby but he was not just for the Jewish people, but for us all. You and I may not be Jewish; we are what the Jews call 'Gentiles'. The baby here (indicating the figure held alongside) was shown to the Wise Men, who were the first Gentiles to be shown the baby. Those visitors stood for us.

ADULT ADDRESS

The 'star-bearer' and the 'baby' carrier stay within easy reach of the place where the sermon will be preached. Three elderly members of the congregation (if possible those who took parts in the Gospel dramatisation) go to the back of the church and collect the three gifts already prepared and left there: a box wrapped in gold paper; a censer or thurible with burning incense in; and a small ornate, Eastern-looking jar or vase. The star-bearer walks to the back of the church to lead the three with the gifts forward. (There is no need for the 'Magi' to be dressed up.) The 'baby' carrier comes to the front step, into the sanctuary, and with the minister on his right stands facing the congregation and the advancing procession.

The adult address begins before the procession moves off from the rear:

Gifts usually express the sentiments 'I love you' or

'Thank you'. These gifts which now approach say neither; they are prophetic gifts. That means that they look to the future, to the roles which this very special baby will fulfil.

There is the gift of gold, for this baby will be a king. Remember the words of Pontius Pilate at Christ's final trial, 'You are a king, then' (John 18:37). He is Christ, our king, who expects our loyalty and devotion.

There is the gift of incense, associated with temple worship and priesthood. This baby will be a priest, offering himself on the altar of the cross. 'He sacrificed ... once for all when he offered himself' (Hebrew 7:27). He is Christ, our priest, who expects us to offer ourselves with him to the glory of the Father.

There is the gift of myrrh, a symbol of suffering and death. This baby is destined to suffer; he will be the Suffering Servant of God. 'He was despised and rejected by men, a man of sorrows, and familiar with suffering' (Isaiah 53:3). He is Christ, our model in the service of others.

Candlemas

BACKGROUND NOTES

This day, 2nd February, is the natural climax of forty days of the Christmas/Epiphany season. Luke, the evangelist, closes his collection of nativity stories with the presentation of the child Jesus in the Temple, the purification of Mary, and the meeting which took place between Mary with the child and the saintly Simeon. Because the day encompasses all three happenings, no other ancient Christian festival has changed its name so many times over the centuries.

This day was first kept about AD 350 by the Christians

of Jerusalem. By 542 it had spread throughout Europe and was then known as 'The Meeting' (Hypapante), referring to the meeting of Simeon and the child Jesus. In the ninth century, when devotion to the Virgin Mary was widespread, it became known as 'The Purification' of Mary. And a little later it was called 'Candlemas' because candles were blessed and distributed at the Mass. This was to call to mind the words of Simeon, 'a light for revelation to the Gentiles'. In more modern times it has been understood as a feast of the Lord, marking the end of the Christmas/Epiphany period and looking ahead to the soon-to-be-celebrated sufferings and death of Jesus.

BIBLICAL NOTE

Between verses 21 and 24 of chapter 2 of his Gospel, Luke, the Gentile writer, jams in three Jewish religious ceremonies: the naming of Jesus at his circumcision, the ritual purification of Mary after childbirth as required by Leviticus 12, and the presentation of the infant Jesus, as the firstborn male child, to God, as required by Exodus 13:2.

Then follows the meeting between the child and Simeon, the righteous Jew, and his recognition of Jesus as the Messiah, 'the light for revelation to the Gentiles'. These words are closely followed by 'a sword will pierce your own soul too'. This is the attraction of Candlemas today; not only does it mark the end of that circle of worship which began five weeks before on the first Sunday of Advent, but it also points us on to Lent and Easter.

VISUAL/DECORATION

The two predominant liturgical colours today are white (to mark the link with the Christmas period) and purple (for the coming of the Lenten season). It is not a good time of the year for flowers, particularly purple ones, so other materials or fabrics can be used. A large display, close to the altar or beneath the pulpit, could use the three Epiphany figures, a large white candle, and two lengths of fabric, one white and one purple. Either drape the white (on the left as seen by the congregation) and the purple side by side over a raised mound and stand the candle in the centre; or drape the material round the foot of a large candlestick.

Place the three Magi figures round the candle, on the draped material as in adoration of the candle (Christ the light of the world). A card with the lettering 'Christ the light of the world' or 'A light for revelation to the Gentiles' might be added.

EXPLORING THE THEME

There are several related themes to be found in this day's celebration. There is purification, presentation, meeting of the old and new covenants, light of the world. Joy and sorrow are to be found; the joy of Simeon and Anna's greeting, but the sorrow in the words of Simeon's prophecy, 'a sword will pierce your own soul too'.

This day brings to an end the Christmas period, when the birth of Christ the Light of the world has been celebrated; the powers of darkness will triumph, briefly, in the coming season of the passion and death of Christ. The most appropriate theme then for our service is Christ the Light of the world, 'the light for the revelation to the Gentiles'.

MUSIC

The music could include some of the following (numbers from *Mission Praise*):

Any arrangement of 'Nunc Dimittis'
The Light of Christ (652)
Like a candle flame (420)
Colours of Day

READINGS

Exodus 12:51; 13:2, 11–16: Consecrate the first born to me.
Leviticus 12:6–8: The Law of Purification.
Isaiah 6:1–8: I saw the Lord fill the Temple.
Haggai 2:1–9: I will fill his house with splendour.
Luke 2:22–40: The Presentation.

INTRODUCTION

The traditional practice is to have a procession at the beginning of this service, which may or may not include the blessing of the candles carried by the congregation. It is most appropriate to gather everyone in a place separate from the church; perhaps in an adjoining hall. There the minister greets everyone and addresses them:

Forty days ago we celebrated the joyful feast of the birth of Jesus, our Lord. Today we recall the day on which he was presented in the Temple, fulfilling the law of Moses... We recall especially the prophetic words of Simeon, 'a light for revelation to the Gentiles'. To commemorate these words and those of Jesus himself later in his life, 'I am the Light of the World', we carry lighted candles into the church, while we sing the words of Simeon (Nunc Dimittis).

The minister may now wish to bless the candles that the people are holding, with these or similar words:

Creator God, source of all light,
today you revealed to Simeon
your light of revelation to the nations.
Bless these candles; may we who carry them
praise your glory and walk in the light
of your love. Amen.

The minister, carrying his own candle, leads the procession into the church.

The procession can wind its way around the church before the people file into their places. The candles are extinguished and the service then continues as usual.

BEFORE THE GOSPEL READING

The minister invites the oldest and the youngest person in each pew, or line of seats, to come out; only the older people bring their candles, which are lit when they reach the front of the church. (It would be as well to give warning of this before the service begins.) The child and the older person need not be of the same family or know one another. The 'couples' are invited to stand side by side close to where the Gospel is to be read. The minister introduces the reading with mention of the ancient name for this feast day, 'The Meeting' (see background note).

That is the meeting between the young Messiah, represented by the young people, and Simeon, represented by the older persons.

AFTER THE GOSPEL READING

The minister invites those representing Simeon to present their lighted candles to their younger companions. The minister then says (if appropriate): At your baptism you were given a lighted candle like this, with the words... As Christ Jesus was a light to the nations, so must we give a shining example of really good, kind behaviour to others, so that they are drawn to be followers of Jesus, too.

The candles are now extinguished and all return to their seats.

ALL-AGE ADDRESS

The minster goes and stands by the 'decoration' (see above) if there is one, or takes a large lighted candle in his hand, then says:

Children always like candles. Is it the attraction of the unusual, the fascination with fire, the element of danger? Most of us never see a flame, like this one, lighting up a room. To us, with our bright fluorescent electric lights, a candle seems to give a very weak light. In the Science Museum in London they used to have a series of show cases showing how light has been used in homes. It started with the fires of the cavemen, the candles of the Middle Ages, through the oil lamps to the gas lights of the Victorians and on to the modern electric lights brightly shining in all our homes. But when you sit in the dark, the lighting of a candle can bring hope and joy.

Imagine living in a country where for two whole months it never gets light. Every day it remains pitch black; there's not a glimmer of light to mark the difference between day and night. That is how it is for the children of the town of Tromso in Norway, every year. Listen to this passage from a newspaper report:

Somewhere behind the dark clouds, something stirred. One hundred and eighty brightly dressed children stared hopefully at the distant, dark horizon.

This was Tromso, Norway – 215 miles inside the Arctic Circle and for the past two months in permanent darkness. Now, at eight minutes to midday, the sun was due back. Not for long, mind you – four minutes only on the first day. But it was enough to bring out a fair proportion of the 50,000 inhabitants of this, the world's most northerly city.

The bells pealed out and hundreds of colourful balloons were sent flying high into the gloom. They had been looking forward to this moment since last November 25th, when the wan winter sun had finally sunk and day had become night. For children, Sun Day – a celebration declared by King Olva in 1873 – means a day off school. One girl said, 'I'm so happy today. If you haven't lived through such a winter as ours, you can't imagine what it's like.'

I couldn't, could you? Nor could anyone imagine what a difference the birth of Christ would make; how wonderfully he would be the light of the nations.

Today is a special day because we can look back to the joy of Christmas (the white of our decoration) when the Light of the World was born; and forward (the purple) to the coming attempt by some to extinguish the Light by a brutal passion and death. As older people will know, life is made up of the white and the purple and we need to keep our Christian light burning through both.

CONCLUDING NOTE

If it is a eucharistic service the children who are not confirmed and have not yet approached the sacrament could be invited to come up, to stand with candles alight around the altar (or suitable place) while Communion is distributed. The minister might like to explain this action in these or similar words:

As we celebrate today the meeting of Simeon with the

infant Messiah, it is fitting that our own 'meeting' with Christ in this sacrament should be illuminated by the welcoming lights of our children.

If desired the children can wait to leave, holding their lighted candles, in the procession of ministers as it leaves the sanctuary.

Lent

BACKGROUND NOTE

The English word Lent, which means 'spring', does not express the significance of the six weeks of spiritual discipline in preparation for Easter. The fasting associated with Lent began with just six days (what we now know as Holy Week), but had been extended by five weeks by the time of the Council of Nicea in AD 325. The longer period was primarily necessary as it was a period of training and preparation for those who were to be baptized on Easter night. As fasting was never allowed on the Lord's Day (which celebrated the Resurrection), Sundays are not included in the forty days from Ash Wednesday to Easter.

BIBLICAL NOTE

Forty is the number traditionally associated with preparation, training and discipline. Jesus spent forty days and nights in the wilderness preparing for his ministry (Matthew 4:2). The Israelites were in the desert for forty years being shaped into God's people fit for the Promised Land (Exodus 16:35). Before God revealed himself to Elijah, the prophet had to travel for forty days and nights. Jonah gave the Ninevites forty days in which to fast and repent.

The ashes used by many to mark the commencement of the forty days is also very biblical; see the king of Nineveh (Jonah 3:6) and Job's repentance (Job 42:6). Jesus himself refers to the need for such signs of repentance (Matthew 11:21).

VISUAL/DECORATION

Lent is traditionally a time when the church remains undecorated with flowers, to fit the sombre nature of the season and to highlight the joy that follows. This does not exclude the use of other teaching visuals. The themes, spoken of in the section on Lent and Holy Week: An Offering of Love, in chapter 3, can be illustrated in poster work by the younger members of the church community and exhibited. There are also poster sets available (eg. Turvey Abbey material, see Appendix 1).

EXPLORING THE THEME

Several themes are interwoven in Lent. There is preparation for the central mystery of our faith; coping with temptation; conflict; suffering; reconciliation and renewal. For the individual it is an opportunity to face reality and the truth about oneself, to critically examine one's life and see if God's will is truly being sought and followed.

We shall prepare well for Easter if, like Jesus, we seek to do God's will, for to do that we have to face the truth about ourselves and deal with the temptations and the conflict involved, which lead to a need for reconciliation and a fresh start.

In the Jewish tradition the story of Jonah is used at times of repentance and reconciliation. Jesus himself made a link between the story of Jonah and Easter (Matthew 12:38–42). In this service we shall follow that example.

MUSIC

Any music and hymns of a penitential nature are suitable, such as the following (numbers from *Mission Praise*):

Abba Father (3)
Amazing Grace (31)
Cleanse me from my sin, Lord (82)
Forty days and forty nights (160)
Do not be afraid (115)
God forgave my sin (181)

READINGS

Each Sunday of Lent has its own set readings for Anglican and Roman Catholic churches but to use the theme of this service the following are most appropriate:

First reading: Book of Jonah, chapters 1 and 2.
Second reading: Matthew 12:38–42.

INTRODUCTION

The preparations for this service depend on how much trouble the planning team want to go to; there can be a simple or a more involved version. For the simple service, choose a cross-section of the congregation to take parts in the reading, so that it is just a straightforward part-reading.

The more involved and more satisfying version would be to act out the reading, with props. A group of the young people (as distinct from the children) can be invited to build a boat using cardboard boxes and other materials on one side of the sanctuary and paint the outline of a big fish on a large sheet of card, behind which 'Jonah' can duck, with his voice only heard. One of the church's youth groups might get involved in this as a Lenten project in the week prior to the service. Of course the actors will have to be rehearsed.

INTRODUCTORY ADDRESS

So that all present will see the point of the play or part-reading which will take place at the usual time for the first reading, the minister needs to spend just a few minutes, either before the entry or first hymn or immediately afterwards, explaining the Lenten themes to be explored in this service.

Use a music group or taped music to provide suitable instrumental music, eg. for the story, to enhance the dramatic presentation. An experienced choir director might find some suitable choral music for the same purpose.

THE PARTS

This is *not* a dramatised reading for the children to perform for the adults. All the parts must be shared out equally across the various age ranges. For example, Jonah could be a teenager and the ship's captain could be an older man; the crew can include females of any age; the narrator should be a woman.

The Man Who Ran Away

An introduction is given by the minister or the narrator. Our story is of the reluctant, and very human, prophet Jonah. It is from that book of the Bible named after him, and it was probably written about 600 years before the birth of Jesus. It is not intended that we think of it as history, it is meant to be a parable, like the stories that

Jesus told. Now a parable is a story that illustrates an idea; it is a story with a meaning.

When the Jewish people celebrate Yom Kippur, the Day of Atonement, they fast all day to express sorrow for their sins. In the synagogue in the afternoon they read the Book of Jonah and apply it to themselves. Being Jewish, Jesus and the first Christians would have been familiar with this practice, which we are going to imitate in this service.

A Jewish rabbi would point out to his congregation how Jonah tried to run away from God, turned his back, and in other words, sinned. This is expressed in the text by the word 'down', which is repeated continually, as you will notice.

Narrator:	The word of Lord came to Jonah. The message was clear.
God:	Go at once to the great city of Nineveh. I have heard of the people's wickedness and you are to tell them to repent.
Narrator:	Jonah did not want to hear or do what he was asked. Instead he ran away.
Jonah:	I'll go to Spain instead. If I go down to Joppa I can find a ship to take me to Tarshish.
Narrator:	So Jonah ignored the Lord and went down to Joppa. He paid his fare and went on board ship.
Jonah:	This ship is going in the opposite direction to Nineveh, so I can't be made to go.
Narrator:	They were only a few days on their journey when the Lord caused a great wind to blow upon the sea and a terrible storm blew up. It was so bad that the captain and the crew

	thought the ship was going to break up under the lashing waves and cruel wind.
Various members of the crew.	a. We're going to drown.
	b. Poseidon, god of the sea, save us.
	c. I've never seen waves like these, we're going to go down.
	b. Save us, mighty Poseidon, save us.
	c. Mighty Zeus, Zeus of wind and weather, save us.
Captain:	Stop the praying and get this deck cargo overboard. Throw over all the heavy tackle. Get a move on.
Narrator:	Meanwhile Jonah had gone down into the hold, where he lay down and fell asleep. The captain, looking for cargo to throw overboard, found Jonah, asleep down in the hold.
Captain:	How can you sleep at a time like this? Get up and pray to your god for help. If you pray hard perhaps your god will be kind and we will not all die.
Narrator:	The sailors meanwhile were trying to find out who had brought such a terrible punishment on the ship.
Sailor A:	You're always unlucky, Jason, it must be your fault.
Sailor B: (Jason)	No, it's not. Let's draw lots to find out whose fault it is.
Narrator:	So they drew straws or cast lots and, yes, it was clear that Jonah was to blame. They said to him:
Sailor B:	Who are you?
Sailor A:	Where are you from?

Sailor C: What nationality are you?

Sailor A: What dreadful thing have you done to bring this punishment on all of us?

Jonah: I am a Hebrew; and we worship the one true God. We believe that he made the whole world, the sea and the sky.

Narrator: The captain and crew, gathered round, were terrified when they heard this.

Captain: What have you done, then, to upset your God?

Narrator: When the sailors heard from Jonah that he was running away from what the Lord God had asked him to do, they asked:

Captain: What must we do to make up to your God and stop this dreadful storm?

Jonah: There's only one thing to do. Throw me overboard, then the sea will become calm again.

Narrator: The sailors did not want to do this and decided to try rowing with the large sea oars that they had. They struggled hard in the torrential rain for hours and then gave up. Faced with the prospect of throwing Jonah over the side, the Captain prayed.

Captain: O please Lord, do not let us all die because of this one man. May we not be found guilty of killing an innocent person. You, O Lord, by your own will, have brought all this about.

Narrator: So the crew heaved Jonah over the side, and he sank down into the lashing waves. Hardly had he disappeared when the wind eased, the waves stopped hammering the ship and the storm passed. The captain and the crew were amazed and set about immediately to offer a sacrifice to the one true God.

Meanwhile Jonah had sunk down in the sea and a huge fish swallowed him alive. He remained there, deep in the fish's belly, for three days and three nights.

Now, at last, when he was as low as he could get, Jonah prayed.

Jonah: In my trouble I called to you Lord,
And you answered me;
From the depths of the grave
I called for help,
And you listened to my cry.
You hurled me into the deep,
Into the heart of the sea,
the currents swirled about me;
all your waves and breakers
swept over me.
I thought I was driven away
out of your sight.
But you brought my life
up from the pit, O Lord my God.
When my life was ebbing away,
I remembered you, Lord,
and my prayer came before you.
What I have promised, I will perform.
Salvation comes from the Lord.

Narrator: The Lord commanded the fish, and it vomited Jonah on to dry land. When God spoke again to Jonah, asking him to go to Nineveh, he obeyed immediately and set off for that great city.

After the reading of the Gospel (Matthew 12:38–42 the children aged under twelve can be taken aside (to the hall or vestry) during the address to learn the following action song (to the tune of London Bridge). They will sing it and lead the congregation in the actions when they return immediately following the sermon.

The song goes to the tune of 'London Bridge', and it is easy to work out accompanying actions. The children's leader can either work out some beforehand or, better still, get the children to suggest ideas.

> Jonah tried to run away,
> Run away, run away;
> Jonah tried to run away,
> Far, far away.
>
> Jonah tried to sail away,
> Sail away, sail away;
> Jonah tried to sail away,
> Far, far away.
>
> Down he went into the sea,
> Into the sea, into the sea;
> Down he went into the sea,
> Down, down, down.
>
> Swallowed alive by a whale,
> By a whale, by a whale;
> Swallowed alive by a whale,
> Down, deep inside.
>
> Jonah prayed in the whale,
> In the whale, in the whale;

Jonah prayed in the whale,
Promised to do better.

On the third day out he came,
Out he came, out he came;
On the third day out he came,
To obey his God.

ADDRESS

The words of Jesus, 'As Jonah was three days and three
nights in the belly of a huge fish, so the Son of Man will
be three days and three nights in the heart of the earth',
link our dramatised first reading with Easter. There is much
in the Jonah story to show us the meaning and purpose of
Lent.

Mothering Sunday

BACKGROUND NOTE

This is celebrated on the fourth Sunday of Lent, which is
often the nearest Sunday to 25th March, the feast of the
Annunciation. From quite early times this feast day, nine
months before Christmas Day, was chosen to celebrate the
motherhood of Mary, and by association this came to be a
celebration of motherhood in general. So the custom has
developed of Mothers Day with visits and gifts for all
mothers.

BIBLICAL NOTE

The text of the event that we call the Annunciation, when
Mary conceived, is found in Luke 1:26–38. Another text,

which is more appropriate for use in Lent, is John 19:25–27.

VISUAL/DECORATION

Women's groups such as Young Wives and Mothers' Union should be invited weeks before to take responsibility for the decoration of the church on this day. The aim is not just to make the church look attractive but to explore, in any medium they wish (within reason), the concept of 'Motherhood'. Hopefully they would not need reminding that the theme should include mothers of teenagers and grandmothers (all-age motherhood).

EXPLORING THE THEME

Pastorally this day is important because of its wide popular appeal, echoed in the secular world. Coming towards the end of Lent it cuts across the penitential nature of the season. This can either be ignored, in view of the wider pastoral implications (Mark 2:27), or the theme can include the suffering of Mary (and by implication all mothers), as the Passion approaches.

It should on the other hand not be a bland 'thank you for mums' day; the original connection with Mary the mother of Jesus should be retained.

MUSIC

The following are suitable (numbers from *Mission Praise*):

Abba Father (3)
For the beauty of the earth (152)
Father I place into your hands (133)
I will sing, I will sing (313)
Now thank we all our God (486)

He's got the whole world (225)

Love divine (449)

READINGS

Select from the following:

Genesis 1:26–28, 31a	Genesis 2:4–9, 15–24
Genesis 23:1–4, 19	1 Samuel 1:20–28
Ruth 1:8–17, 22	Proverbs 31:10–31
2 Timothy 1:3–10	Ephesians 5:26–6:4
Matthew 7:21, 24–27	John 19:23–29
Luke 1:26–28	Luke 11:1–13
Mark 10:2–16	

ALTERNATIVE READING

The following comes from that celebrated writer, 'Author Unknown'.

When God was creating mothers, he was deep in his sixth day of overtime. An angel appeared and said, 'You're doing a lot of fiddling around on this one.' And God answered, 'Look at the requirement on this order and you'll understand why. She has to be completely washable but not plastic. Have 180 movable parts, each one replaceable. Run on black coffee and leftovers. Have a kiss that can cure anything from a broken leg to a disappointed love affair. And have six pairs of hands.'

The angel shook her head, 'Six pairs of hands? That's not possible even for you, O God.' 'It's not the hands that are causing me problems,' replied the Lord. 'It's the three pairs of eyes that mothers are supposed to have.' Asked the angel, 'Are the three pairs of eyes supposed to be on the standard model?' The Lord nodded gravely. 'One pair that sees through closed doors when she asks, "What are you kids doing in there?" – even though she already knows. Another pair in the back of her head that sees what she shouldn't but what she has to know. And of course the ones here in front that can look at a child when he goofs and reflect, "I understand and I love you," even though she doesn't utter a word.'

'Lord,' said the angel, touching his sleeve gently, 'come to bed. Tomorrow ... try again.' 'I can't,' said the Lord. 'I'm so close to creating something so similar to myself. Already I have one who heals herself when she is sick, can feed a family of six on one pound of hamburger, and get a nine-year-old to stay under a shower for an incredible two minutes.'

The angel circled the model of the mother very slowly and sighed, 'It's much too soft, dear God.' 'Soft, yes, but tough too,' said the Lord excitedly. 'You cannot imagine what the mother can do or endure.' Asked the angel 'Can it think?' 'Not only think,' said the Creator. 'It can also reason and compromise.'

Finally the angel bent over and ran her fingers across the cheek. 'There's a leak,' she said suddenly. 'I told you that you were trying to put too much into this model. You can't ignore the stress factor.'

The Lord moved in for a closer look and gently lifted the drop of moisture to his finger where it glistened and sparkled in the light. 'It's not a leak,' God said. 'It's a tear.' The angel queried, 'A tear? What's that for?' 'It's for joy, sadness, disappointment, compassion, pain, loneliness, and pride.' 'You are a genius,' said the angel rapturously.

The Lord looked sombre and said, 'I didn't put it there.'

INTRODUCTION

The giving of flowers is associated with Mothering Sunday. As the congregation enter, young children (rehearsed to do this) can offer a small bunch (three or four flowers) or a single daffodil to each mother (including, of course, grandmothers). Just before the service begins the mothers can be invited to come forward with their flowers to place them in flower vases arranged in a letter M. At the end of the service the mothers are invited to come forward to receive back their flowers, to take home. After the flowers have been put in the vases, the minister can explain that the M stands for Mary, whose Annunciation and motherhood we are celebrating; and equally the M stands for the motherhood of all those who placed their flowers in the vases.

ADDRESS

The alternative reading could be read by a teenager at this point. (It is especially relevant for a teenager to do this because of the regular friction that can occur between mothers and their teenage offspring.)

The speaker can comment on the humorous portrait of the model mother and how tough mothers must be for their demanding job. Mothers like to say 'yes' to their children. Sometimes if mistakes are made it is because they say 'yes' too often; there is always the danger of spoiling a child. Mary, the mother of our saviour, said 'yes' to God on the day we are celebrating, nine months before Christmas Day. She accepted God's will for her: 'May it be to me as you have said' (Luke 1:38).

Serving a family not only involves saying 'yes' to others continually, but so often means saying 'no' to oneself.

Today we say 'thank you' to all mothers for all the sacrifices they have made for the sake of their families.

Easter

BACKGROUND NOTE

Easter is the greatest and oldest festival and the central focus of our faith. Its importance is emphasised by the long preparation of Lent, Passiontide and the special ceremonies of Holy Week. According to the Anglo-Saxon Church historian, the Venerable Bede, the name 'Easter' originates from the pagan goddess of spring, Eostre.

In the first three centuries it was a commemoration of the cross and resurrection. An evolution began in the fourth century with the development of Good Friday and the limiting of the Pascha, the Christian Passover, to the Sunday.

The secular world, in modern times, has made more and more of Christmas for commercial reasons, while it has made less and less of Good Friday and Easter Sunday. But for chocolate eggs, Easter would pass unnoticed by society, and ministers and pastoral leaders have to work hard to re-affirm the centrality and vital importance of this festival of the Lord's death and resurrection.

BIBLICAL NOTE

The Gospel narrative makes it abundantly clear that Jesus deliberately chose the season of the Passover to go up to the Holy City and confront his critics, the Jewish authorities. At the festival celebrating the central event of the Old Covenant, the escape from slavery, Jesus gives a New Covenant, sealed in his blood (Luke 22:20). This final celebration of the Passover, the Last Supper, stands at the decisive frontier between, on the one side, the Jewish Passover and the Old Covenant, and on the other side, the annual

celebration of the Christian Passover and the weekly celebration of the Christian Eucharist.

VISUAL/DECORATION

As with Christmas, churches have their own traditions
about Easter which need to be questioned from time to
time to see if they still 'work'.

'Festive' and 'Joyful' are the themes as we celebrate new
life. The flower arrangements should radiate the life and
excitement of the wondrous miracle of the Lord's conquest
over death. If an Easter garden is considered, why not go
for a life-size one? If there are pillars and window-sills,
these can be shared out among the church groups, not
forgetting the children and young people's groups. Give
each a theme: Risen to Life – Light and Life – Born Again
– Waters of Life, etc.

EXPLORING THE THEME

This could be called the Service of the Three Gardens.
The clue is from Paul's insight: 'Adam was a pattern of the
one to come ... through the disobedience of the one man
the many were made sinners ... through the obedience
of the one man...' (Romans 5). And again, 'As in Adam
all die, so in Christ all will be made alive' (1 Corinthians
15:22). Obedience is the key which links the Garden of
Eden, the Garden of Gethsemane and the Garden of the
Empty Tomb.

In the Garden of Eden (however interpreted) we see the
first human sin, the sin of disobedience: humans were not
prepared to do God's will.

In the Garden of Gethsemane Jesus pleads, Please do
not ask this suffering of me ... but not my will, your will
be done. The second Adam accepts God's will.

In the Garden of the Tomb, the Father shows the whole human race that he accepts nothing but simple obedience – 'thy will be done on earth as it is in heaven' – and the obedience of Jesus is rewarded with his Resurrection. He is established as Lord and Christ (Acts 2:36).

MUSIC

Select from the following (numbers in *Mission Praise*):

Rejoice the Lord is risen (576)
Alleluia, give thanks (30)
Jesus Christ is risen today (357)
Christ the Lord is risen (76)
In the tomb (340)
This is the day (691)
Low in the grave (453)
In the tomb so cold (340)
I know that my Redeemer lives (278)
Thine be the glory (689)

The choir could sing:

Love is come again (Oxley)
Ye choirs of New Jersualem (Stanford)

READINGS

The Easter readings are provided in the liturgical books. If this Service of the Three Gardens is to be followed, the following are suitable:
Genesis 3:1–13
1 Corinthians 5:12–22
Mark 14:32–38 followed by Mark 16:1–7

INTRODUCTION

The theme is deeply theological and is the very basis of the Christian Faith. Participants will benefit according to their own place on the faith journey. Children may only see that there is a link between the Garden of Eden and the death and resurrection of Jesus, but even that is a success to be built on in the future. More experienced adults may be prompted to meditate upon their need to seek God's will more faithfully in their lives.

To communicate the connection between the three gardens of the theme, the planning group could arrange for three gardens, static displays, to be provided (each one could be the responsibility of a different church group). The largest should be the Resurrection display. A large scale tomb could be built with live guards asleep outside and real women visiting; such a tableau has been known to work very well.

Alternatively there could be three mini-plays, each before or after (or in place of) the reading. Or select three part-readings from *The Dramatised Bible.*

Prepare three large white cards. On one draw a large apple, on another a butterfly, and the last an olive tree or an owl.

Before the service commences or as part of the introductory rites, the minister shows the cards one by one. (Young people can hold the cards up for the minister.)

Apple: In the Garden of Eden Eve took the fruit from the tree and shared it with Adam. The fruit has traditionally been represented by the apple.

Olive tree or owl: In the Garden of Gethsemane or the Garden of Olives, where Jesus prayed in agony before his

Passion, there are olive trees. It was night time when Jesus prayed in agony, and someone must have seen and recorded what happened, like a wise old owl.

Butterfly: In the Garden of the Empty Tomb there would have been butterflies. The butterfly has been a symbol of the Resurrection since the early years of Christianity.

READINGS

The readings should be dramatically presented (see Introduction above).

CHILDREN'S ADDRESS

Return to the cards with the three symbols. Each one can be held up by a child and more fully explained, this time linking the apple with the other two. Because Adam and Eve did not do as they were told, they took the apple. In the garden full of olive trees Jesus prayed, he then said 'yes' to what God his Father asked him – the opposite of what Adam and Eve did in their garden. The butterfly emerges from the apparently dead chrysalis to a beautiful new life. The Father rewards Jesus for saying 'yes' to him.

CHILDREN'S ACTIVITY

During the adult sermon, the children are asked to select an adult to go with them to a separate place (encourage them not to choose a parent). They are to talk with the adult about 'How we can be like Jesus and not like Adam' (that is, obedient to God's will). Then express this in a drawing or picture.

ADULT ADDRESS

'Thy Kingdom come, thy will be done.' We pray this regularly, but have we understood what we are saying? God's kingdom of love, here and now, and in the future, can only come about by our doing what God asks, here and now.

Adam failed to do God's will and the consequence was mankind's separation from God. The second Adam, after a struggle, was obedient. Notice, 'after a struggle': Jesus had prayed, 'Take this suffering away ... but your will be done.' His struggle and his obedience were rewarded. He was raised, and established as Lord and Christ. Jesus is the man in whom the kingdom has come, because he did God's will.

Only by finding and trying hard to do God's will – it is sometimes a big struggle – will the Kingdom come for us and in us.

The children return in procession and present their work to the minister, who shares it with the congregation.

Pentecost

BACKGROUND NOTE

The Greek word for Pentecost refers to the fiftieth day, being the period of time from the Passover to one of the pilgrim festivals of the Old Covenant, which celebrated the wheat harvest.

Until the fourth century Christians celebrated on this day both the Ascension of the Lord and the coming of the Holy Spirit. In the course of the fourth century a separate day was introduced as Ascension Day, and then Pentecost was given over solely to the descent of the Holy Spirit.

The word Whitsun is derived from White Sunday, which

was the last day on which those who had been baptized at Easter wore their white baptismal tunics or robes.

BIBLICAL NOTE

Pentecost is the birthday of the Church. 'It was not the brain-child of the disciples; it was the work of God. God spoke to its founder members and worked among them in such power that they had no option but to respond to his orders' (John Drane). Acts 2:1–12 speaks of that 'religious experience' that is best described as 'what seemed to be tongues of fire', a descriptive metaphor very appropriate to what was just about to happen, in the first proclamation of the Good News.

VISUAL/DECORATION

The predominant colour for the flower arrangements should be red, but orange and yellow can also contribute to remind everyone of the tongues of fire.

If the design and layout of the church permit, that is, if there are twelve pillars (six on either side) or twelve wall spaces, mount twelve identical posters. They should be at least A3 size, with a very large bright red and yellow flame shape, and can be made by the young people.

A good idea is to announce two weeks before Whitsun (and remember to explain the idea in the newsletter) that all churchgoers, of every age, are invited to bring a small gift wrapped in red paper on Pentecost morning. Guidance will need to be given about the mystery gift, stating that none should cost more than £2, to avoid embarrassing those who cannot afford much. The planning team may decide to give guidance about the type of gift, eg. a small box of chocolates; a small dried-flower arrangement; a homemade badge or brooch from modelling material. The team could also buy a small number of gifts which will be wrapped and ready at the back of the church, available for any person who turns up on Pentecost Sunday unprepared.

Either after an introductory word by the minister/leader at the commencement of the service or after the Gospel reading, the congregation are asked to leave their places and present their gift to someone they do not know, or do not know very well. (The Spirit of Love makes us all members of one another.)

Another idea is to ask all church members to attend that day wearing something red.

EXPLORING THE THEME

Any of the symbols of Pentecost can be taken and developed. (See 'The Pentecost: The Giving of Love' in chapter 3.) Here we are using the symbol of fire.

MUSIC

Choose from the following (numbers in *Mission Praise*):

Come Holy Ghost (90)
Come down, O love divine (89)
Gracious Spirit (198)
Spirit of God divine (610)
Spirit of holiness (611)
Spirit of the living God (612/613)
Spirit Divine (614)
The Spirit lives (664)

The choir could sing:

Christ is the world's true light (Stanton)
O Lord, give thy Holy Spirit (Tallis)

READINGS

Readings for Pentecost are:

Genesis 11:1–9

Acts 2:1–11

1 Corinthians 12:3–7, 12–13

John 20:19–23 or John 14:15–26

Where possible use *The Dramatised Bible* with the Acts passage. A dramatic effect can be achieved by building up a cacophany of noise. The young people would enjoy doing this at the back of the church. (Warn the rest of the congregation that it is part of the service and not some disrespectful behaviour!) The talking can start quietly and build up. At the words in Acts 2, verse 11, 'We hear them declaring the wonders of God in our own tongues,' all noise stops. Everyone then reads or says together, 'The Spirit unites us in the language of love.' Or without any introduction the hymn 'The Spirit lives' is sung.

INTRODUCTION

In the 'Visual' section it was suggested that at the service two weeks before this one all the congregation should be invited to wear something red for this service and/or bring a small gift to present to someone they do not know. This could take place after the Gospel, when a link can be made with God's free gift of His Spirit to us, and how this gift leads us into loving service.

Four volunteers are required: an elderly man, a teenage boy, a small girl and a middle-aged mother. Each is to prepare a few words about fire. The man could speak of using a bonfire in his garden to burn rubbish. The boy might speak perhaps of his achievement as a scout of lighting a fire with one match, or describe fraternity around a campfire. The small girl may speak of how she has been warned of the dangers of playing with matches, or of her fear of fire. The mother could talk about cooking on an open fire on some occasion, or on a gasfire.

ADDRESS

After the Gospel the four 'volunteers' come forward. The minister then speaks of the symbolism of the colour red, related to the 'fire' of the Holy Spirit. The four people then make their presentation. The minister proceeds to the qualities of fire: fire as a cleansing power; fire which gives light; fire which can frighten; the warmth of fire, etc. The coming of the Holy Spirit lit up the minds of the Apostles and warmed their hearts with love.

The same can happen to us if we welcome the Spirit. All the ancient hymns to the Holy Spirit begin with the word 'Veni' (Come), and that must be our constant prayer: 'Come, Holy Spirit, enlighten our minds and warm our hearts by the fire of your love.'

Trinity Sunday

BACKGROUND NOTE

This festival is different in character from those which commemorate the historical events of salvation. It is always held on the first Sunday after Pentecost and it was introduced officially as part of the Church calendar in the fourteenth century to mark the end of the cycle commemorating the life of Christ and the descent of the Holy Spirit.

The day was especially popular in England, perhaps because Thomas Becket was consecrated bishop on that day in 1162. Formerly, from the ancient Sarum Rite and the Book of Common Prayer, Sundays were reckoned after Trinity and not after Pentecost.

Today it acts as a powerful reminder, if celebrated in a way that really draws it to everyone's attention, that the Christian life is lived for the Father, by the power of the Holy Spirit, through the saving work of Christ our Lord. We are not Unitarians nor so charismatic that we forget the Father and the Son.

Trinity Sunday is the key festival of all-age worship, for it reminds us of the 'community' or 'family' life in God. As this day comes in the early summer, in May or June, it is an ideal weekend on which to have a full day all-age event.

BIBLICAL NOTE

The central dogma of Christian theology is held to be a mystery in the sense that it can neither be known by unaided reason, apart from revelation, nor cogently demonstrated by reason after it has been revealed. The word 'Trinity' (Tri-unity) is not found in the Bible and was first used in the second century; however the teaching is held to be explicit and implicit in Scripture, for example in the baptismal words of Matthew 28:19 and at the baptism of Jesus, Matthew 3:16. The Last Supper speech of Jesus, John 14:11, 16f, expresses the belief very clearly. (See also 1 Peter 1:2 and 2 Corinthians 13:14.)

VISUAL/DECORATION

The creativity of flower arrangers is stretched by this festival which defies the use of the imagination. If three strong colours can be used that remain separate at the top of the arrangement but come to blend together at the bottom, this might convey the right effect.

The most suitable visual is the icon by Andrei Rublev, painted in the fifteenth century and obtainable in poster form (see list of suppliers in appendix 1). If this is used a few minutes should be set aside to give a simple explanation (see *Gateway to the Trinity*, appendix 1).

EXPLORING THE THEME

The inner 'family' life of God is mysterious and unapproachable through the human imagination; however the existence of the human family aids the understanding. A grasp of the simple but profound union of love between husband and wife, made visible in their first child, is as near as anyone can get to this mystery. The human family should therefore be used in this service.

MUSIC

The following are suitable (numbers in *Mission Praise*):

Father, we adore you (139)
Holy, holy (238)
Holy, holy, holy, Lord God (237)
Father God, I love you (129)
Father God, the Lord, Creator (130)

The choir could sing:

Holy, holy, holy (Palestrina)

READINGS

Choose from the following:

Isaiah 6:1–8	2 Corinthians 13:11–13
Exodus 34:4–6, 8–9	John 14:8–17
Deuteronomy 4:32–34,	John 3:16–18
39–40	Matthew 28:16–20
Ephesians 1:3–14	
Romans 8:14–17	

INTRODUCTION

Get together three family groups of mother, father and child. Groups, ideally, should span the age range. For example, the first family group could consist of a young couple with a baby (the younger the better), the second group with a ten-year-old daughter or son, and the last group could be an elderly couple with a grown-up son or daughter. These nine people should be as involved in the service as possible, reading, taking the offerings, etc.

The presentation of the three families could come at the opening of the service or immediately after the Gospel, as an introduction to the sermon or address.

The married couple should stand side by side, with their child in front, between them. The minister introduces the nine people, group by group. The comment could then include the following points.

We have here three families. They have varying ages, but are still the family unit. The baby is totally dependent, the school child is growing in independence and the grown-up is totally independent, yet there is still the bond of family love and mutual respect.

The love of husband and wife for one another is visible to everyone in the existence of the child. In the family of God that we call the Trinity, the total love of the first person (the Father) for the second person (the Word who was made flesh) and the return of that love, is made visible in the Spirit of Love, the third person of the Trinity. So the best image to help humans understand the Trinity is the human family; three examples of which you see before you. (It is advisable to avoid using the term 'Son' of the second person in this explanation, because it will confuse.)

ADDRESS

The ideal visual aid for the sermon or address is the icon by Rublev (it is recommended to read first the very short book, 'Gateway to the Trinity' see appendix!). The family groups, already described, would make an ideal starting point. No attempt at philosophical or theological explanation is desirable; the Trinity as a union of love, similar to the human family, is the most helpful approach. Ordinary family people can enter into the mystery of love without any need for mathematic confusion with talk of one in three and three in one. The numerous Scripture references given above will demonstrate the Holy Trinity in action.

Harvest

BACKGROUND NOTES

Although there were Jewish precedents the Christian Church had no Harvest Festival, as such, until relatively recent history. In England, from Saxon times until the Reformation, there was Lammas (Loaf Mass) on 1st August, with the blessing of bread made from the first ripe corn. In 1843 the Rev. R.S. Hawker, vicar of Morwenstow in Cornwall, revived the Lammas custom and extended the thanksgiving for the whole harvest. The revival spread into the Nonconformist churches and, more recently, the Roman Catholic Church.

BIBLICAL NOTE

The Old Testament called for a celebration called Shavuoth, the Feast of Weeks or Pentecost, to thank God for the first fruits of the harvest. Later, in the autumn, to celebrate the second harvest, the festival of Tabernacles was held (Exodus 23:16, Deuteronomy 16:9, 13). The early Christians do not appear to have commemorated the harvest, perhaps because they were expecting the return of the Lord at any time.

VISUAL/DECORATION

Most churches have their customary way of decorating for this celebration, but it should not become routine. We should not lose sight of our link with the soil, which was expressed more in former times when more churchgoers were agricultural workers. Harvest not only expresses thanks 'up' to God but reminds us of our link, 'down' with the earth and the cycle of the seasons. Gardening tools, spades, forks, rakes, etc can be brought into church and incorporated into vegetable and floral arrangements.

EXPLORING THE THEME

Harvest thanksgiving: there is no 'thanks' without 'giving'. On Mothers Day thanks are expressed by the giving of gifts. The central act of Christian worship, the Eucharist ('Thanksgiving') expresses gratitude to God and involves the gifts of bread and wine and God's gift of his own Son. At Harvest Festival time we say 'thank you' for God's goodness with the gifts we offer for those in need. (Every town and city has homeless people as well as needy elderly.)

MUSIC

Any suitable hymn or song of thanksgiving can be used, such as the following (numbers in *Mission Praise*):

Come, you thankful people, come (106)
For the beauty of the earth (152)
For the fruits of his creation (153)
Praise God from whom all blessing flow (557)
We plough the fields (732)

READINGS

Deuteronomy 8:1–10   Genesis 1:1–3, 24–31a
Acts 14:13–17   Timothy 6:6–10
Luke 12:16–31   John 6:27–35

ALTERNATIVE READING

'Harvest Home', from chapter 15 of *Lark Rise* by Flora Thompson could be read:

At last, in the cool dusk of an August evening, the last load of corn was brought in, with a nest of merry boys' faces among the sheaves on the top of the yellow and blue painted farm wagons drawn by the big cart-horses and the men walking alongside with pitchforks on their shoulders. As they passed along the roads they shouted, 'Harvest home. Harvest home. Merry, merry, merry, harvest home,' and women came to their cottage gates and waved, and the few passers-by looked up and smiled their congratulations. The joy and pleasure of the labourers in their task well done... They loved the soil and rejoiced in their work and skill in bringing forth the fruits of the soil, and 'harvest home' put the crown on their year's work.

INTRODUCTION

It would be interesting to try to dramatise the passage from *Lark Rise*, using people of all age groups and bringing out the huge difference between harvest celebrations of a century ago in England and today. One option is to use this passage after the Gospel reading and before the address or sermon, forming part of it.

Before the service people of various ages, who are willing to take part, could be given items bought in the local supermarket. They need to be chosen carefully; the intention is to demonstrate how food that makes up our modern diet comes from many different countries. In contrast one hundred years ago the people could only eat local food that was in season, or had been preserved by methods like salting or pickling.

At the appropriate time those with the grocery items from abroad can be invited to stand and tell everyone what they have and where it comes from. A number of teaching points can be made of this.

Later in the service the same people, of varied ages, could take part in a thank you litany, for example:

Minister:	Lord God, our creator, provider and sustainer, we thank you for all your gifts and for the people who grow, harvest and supply to our shops the food which we buy for our needs.
First person (holding up food item):	We thank you for... (eg. tea from Sri Lanka).
Second person:	We thank you for... (eg. oranges from Israel). *And so on.*

CONCLUDING PRAYER

'Father of All, our cupboards and larders are full of the fruits of the earth from every corner of the world you have given us.

We sincerely thank you for such bounty and ask that those who grow and supply this food for our benefit may receive a just reward for their efforts, so that all your people, rich and poor, may together be able to thank you. Amen.'

OFFERING OF THE GIFTS

Apart from those gifts which are used to decorate the church, the people may be encouraged to bring a gift or gifts for homeless people, the local women's refuge, or a similar local charity. If it is a eucharistic service the ideal time for these to be presented is when the bread and wine are brought to the altar.

The children should not be left to carry the gifts in procession to present them to the minister. This should be an all-age activity, so that the whole community is seen to be represented.

ADDRESS OR SERMON

See Introduction above.

CONCLUSION OF THE SERVICE

A representative of the organistion or group which is to benefit from the gifts could be invited to the service to thank the community.

All Saints

BACKGROUND NOTE

Celebrating Saints' Days and 'All Saints' is yet another way in which the Church celebrates the Paschal (Easter) mystery. Those Christians who have lived, suffered and died as witnesses of the Risen Christ are brought to us as examples, drawing all to the Father through Christ.

So many martyrs and non-martyrs died in the early years, and since, that a common festival was instituted. At the beginning of the fifth century a day for All Martyrs was first observed on Easter Friday. The Easter connection was lost when in AD 835 the feast day was transferred to 1st November, with the title 'All Saints'.

BIBLICAL NOTE

The biblical foundation of this festival is found in the promises of Jesus (Matthew 19:28) to those who have served him. The idea that the dead may intercede for the living is found in the parable of Dives and Lazarus (Luke 16:19–31). The idea of saints as more than past heroes to admire and imitate, but surrounding and supporting us on our pilgrimage, is found in Hebrews 12:1. Revelation speaks particularly of the martyrs in 6:9f and 7:14–17.

However the principal basis of the practice is Paul's teaching of the mystical Body of Christ, in which all members have their particular office (Romans 12:4–8) as fellow citizens with the saints.

VISUAL/DECORATION

In a suitable place, beneath the pulpit or to one side of the altar, a small 'house' can be constructed by the youth group or older children. Made of building blocks of small cardboard boxes, covered in red crepe paper or painted red, with a roof, it need not stand more than about 3ft high. Around it arrange vases of white chrysanthemums. (The colours used must be red and white.)

Before or during the introduction, or as part of the address or sermon, the symbolism of the decoration needs to be explained. Briefly, today is the festival of those who belong to the household of the Christian Faith, those of us who are alive here and now and those who are alive with God. Baptism (the white flowers) unites us all, as children of God. Many in the past, and today in places like the Sudan, have shed their blood for their faith (the red of the house).

Exploring the Theme

This festival is a celebration of the Communion of Saints, or the Mystical Body of Christ. This day does not celebrate canonised saints or make special mention of any of them; today celebrates the good lives of the millions of Christians (of all branches of the Christian family) who are now with God. Particularly we can recall saintly members of our own family and our community. We thank God for the inspiring example of their lives and ask that they will intercede for us with God.

Music

Any hymn or song which brings out the 'family' nature of the Church, such as the following (numbers in *Mission Praise*):

For all the saints (148)
Father, I place into your hands (133)
He's got the whole world (225)
Seek ye first (590)
Soldiers of Christ, arise (604)
Thy hand, O God, has guided (705)
Through all the changing scenes (702)

Readings

Revelation 7:2–4, 9–14   Romans 12:3–9
1 John 3:1–3   1 Corinthians 12:12–13,
Matthew 5:1–12   27–31

Introduction

Make up a list of past members of the community who have been lovingly remembered for their devout life and service to the community. This can be done either by the planning group, or by asking the community in previous weeks for proposed names. (Tact may be necessary to avoid giving offence; the person must have had some recognition within the community.)

Choose representatives of every age group, from the youngest that can walk unaided, to the eldest parishioner.

The names on the list are distributed to those of this group who are old enough to read. The representatives enter with the minister(s) and take part in the introductory part of the service.

After the opening explanation of the visual/decoration, or in place of it, the representatives of the community are introduced. They are then invited, in the name of the local community, to read out the names of honoured past members. The reason for doing this is explained.

INTERCESSIONS

These will be led by the representatives of the community who entered with the minister(s). If it fits the traditions of the community, incense can be used. Live charcoals need to be left standing, in a suitable receptacle (eg. a thurible), before the altar or communion table. Beside it lies a container of incense with a spoon. One of the younger representatives is invited to come forward at the appropriate moment to place a spoonful of incense on the coals.

Reader: 'The twenty-four elders fell down before the Lamb. Each one had a harp and they were holding golden bowls full of incense, which are the prayers of the saints' (Revelations 5:8).

	(Representative steps forward and sprinkles the incense on the coals)
Reader:	'Worthy is the Lamb, who is slain, to receive power and wealth and wisdom and strength and honour and glory and praise' (Revelations 5:12).
Minister:	Almighty Father, we set before you, like incense, our intercessions and offer them to you in the name of the Lamb of God, who ever lives to make intercession to you on our behalf.
Community representative:	For those who lead our church/parish community, may they be inspired by the saintly example of those who have gone before.
Response by all:	May our prayer be set before you like incense (Psalm 141:2).
Community representative:	For those who have been recently baptized or who are preparing for baptism, may the baptized and honoured members of our community who have gone before intercede for them.
Response by all:	May our prayer be set before you like incense.
Community representative:	For our young people, may they receive a good example in living from all the present members of our community and be inspired by the lives of those who have gone before.
Response by all:	May our prayer be set before you like incense.

This format is continued to encompass the needs of the community.

CHILDREN'S ADDRESS

The following simple story is a very effective starting point.

A little girl was with her family in a group of people who were being shown round one of England's great cathedrals. As the guide was explaining an ancient tomb nearby, the girl was staring at a great stained glass window, through which the summer sun was streaming, bathing the cathedral floor in colour. As the group was about to move on she asked in a shrill clear voice, 'Who are those people in the pretty window?'

'Those are the saints,' the guide replied.

That night as she was undressing for bed, she told her mother, 'I know who the saints are.'

'Do you, dear,' replied her mother. 'Who are they?'

'They're the people who let the light shine through.'

Any other address or sermon could well begin with a story or anecdote from the lives of those whose names have been read out.

4

ALL-AGE ACTIVITIES TO
ILLUSTRATE HYMNS

Ideally all worship by a community is all-age worship. In practice this is rarely so. This section offers ideas on how to add a simple all-age dimension to the regular act of worship. Little preparation is necessary, and not all examples involve an action.

All-age activities to illustrate hymns are very useful when there is little time to consult a team and prepare a full service, but there is a desire to provide an all-age dimension to the standard Sunday service. The following suggestions are only guides to help the pastoral practitioner formulate his or her own ideas.

Simple participatory activites are described for the following hymns. They can form part of all-age events, or be slipped in to the regular service to involve everyone present (Numbers in *Mission Praise*).

Abandonment to God	(133)
All God's creatures	(23)
Bread of life	(64)
Christian meditation	(608)
Forgiveness	(181)
God is Love	(187)
God's family	(54)

God's universe	(327)
Holy Spirit	(500)
Individual dignity	(445)
In God's hands	(225)
Jesus, our all	(384)
Jesus, our Saviour	(59)
Joy in living	(577)
Living for God	(624)
Names of God	(142)
Power of good example	(167)
Respecting creation	(7)
Returning to God	(31)
Spiritual growth	(627)
The holy name	(285)
The Lord's Supper	(414)
Trust in God	(115)

ABANDONMENT TO GOD: 'FATHER I PLACE INTO YOUR HANDS' (*Mission Praise* 133)

The previous week, or earlier the same day, the children can do some work on 'Hands', how we use our hands in God's service and to help others. If they have drawn round and coloured their own hands these can be shown to all present. Alternatively, and if the setting is appropriate and the recording available, the old Max Bygraves song 'You need hands', could be played.

If neither of the above is possible or suitable, individuals can be invited to come forward and speak of how their hands are vital in their work, for example a young woman who works all day at a word processor, or a surgeon who operates, or the mother of a large family, or an ambulance man.

After making the link between working with our hands and placing our lives in God's hands, the following prayer of Charles de Foucauld might be copied and given out.

Father,
I abandon myself into your hands;
do with me what you will.
Whatever you may do, I thank you;
I am ready for all, I accept all.
Let only your will be done in me,
and in all your creatures –
I wish no more than this, O Lord.

Into your hands I commend my soul;
I offer it to you with all the love of my heart,
for I love you, Lord,
and so need to give myself,
to surrender myself into your hands,
without reserve, and with boundless confidence,
for you are my father.

After the above has been read together or by one person, the hymn is sung.

ALL GOD'S CREATURES: 'ALL THINGS BRIGHT AND BEAUTIFUL' (*Mission Praise* 23)

This is suitable on the nearest Sunday to 4th October, the feast day of St Francis of Assisi. On the previous Sunday people (not just children) could be encouraged to bring the easy-to-bring pets (like goldfish and hamsters – dogs too if the community is agreeable). Several representative folk can come forward to say a word about their pet, eg.

why it has its name, its age, etc. The minister can choose to say a word about God's creation or read Genesis 2:19-20, with a simple commentary, or incorporate the reading about St Francis on page 148. The hymn may follow.

BREAD OF LIFE: 'BREAK THOU THE BREAD OF LIFE' (*Mission Praise* 64)

The minister needs several different types of bread, loaves, rolls, etc. If possible use unleavened matzos or pitta bread.
   The minister shows them and explains that they are all bread, the staff of life. He then shows the unleavened bread and explains how this is used at the Passover and in Jewish ritual meals. The matzos can be broken up at this point and the children can help to distribute it. The hymn can now be sung.

CHRISTIAN MEDITATION: 'SPEAK, LORD, IN THE STILLNESS' (*Mission Praise* 608)

The minister asks for total silence and stillness. 'Be still and know that I am God'; no music, no movement, a still church. He then asks everyone to sit up straight with backs against the back support, feet apart and hands in laps. (When this is tried in schools, children amazingly like this.) There should be a large lighted candle, a picture or something similar that can act as a focal point. The minister asks everyone to look intently on the focal point and try to hear any sounds that there are in the distance – these must now be rejected. Everyone breathes in slowly, hold, and out slowly ... the familiar meditation routine. Continue for about five minutes, then sing the hymn (or a similar one).

FORGIVENESS: 'GOD FORGAVE MY SIN'
(*Mission Praise* 181)

A long roll of paper (the blank side of spare wallpaper is perfect) is required with the word FORGIVE printed in large letters seven times, one below the other. An adult reader is also required. The minister then comments on how difficult it is to forgive, quoting a topical case; how often should we forgive? The minister holds paper to view and reveals the word FORGIVE. The reader now reads Matthew 18:21-22. The paper is unrolled by young people slowly to reveal all seven words. The last one is followed by a space (suspense) then 'WITHOUT END'. The hymn is then sung.

GOD IS LOVE: 'GOD IS LOVE'
(*Mission Praise* 187)

Collect copies of the cartoons, 'Love is ...' by Kim which are featured in the Daily Mail. (Collections are published in book form.) Distribute them among the congregation, to a mix of ages. Ask each recipient to describe and read out their cartoon. Explain that one of the greatest revelations of the New Testament is found in 1 John 4:8: 'God is love'. So, for a Christian, the answer to the question, 'What is love?' is 'Love is God' or 'God is love'. Christ invited us to share in the very nature of God, by dedicating our lives to loving. The hymn can now be sung.

GOD'S FAMILY: 'BIND US TOGETHER, LORD' (*Mission Praise* 54)

Required for this 'action': a house brick, a cauliflower (or similar vegetable) and a branch from a rose bush (or some similar bush or tree). The minister asks, 'Which is the odd one out?' He encourages replies from all age groups. If no one gets it right – they must have the reason why one is odd – then read John 15:1–8, as a clue.

The answer is the vegetable, because it grows and exists on its own, it is complete in itself. The house brick, however, is intended to form part of a wall and the branch belongs to a whole plant. We too, as Christians, belong to one another, as members of the family of God. The hymn is now sung.

GOD'S UNIVERSE: 'IMMORTAL, INVISIBLE, GOD ONLY WISE' (*Mission Praise* 327)

First the minister asks the young people, 'Have any of you seen a video or film recently about space?' After listening to the replies, the next question, aimed at the adults, is,

'Is there anyone who studies or likes to read about space and astronomy?' Following the response to this, give out these passages to readers of different ages.

A. Let our minds soar. Let us stand in spirit at the margent of the universe and travel in through the galaxies of stars, the clusters of planets, stretching beyond the limits of sight, sown like seed across the plains of darkness.

B. Let us travel at the speed of light, 186,000,000 miles a

second, through 15,000,000,000 light years, past stars
vaster in size than the whole of our own solar system,
through unimaginable distance, unimaginable fire and
cold, searching for that speck we call our world, like a
speck of sand upon the ocean bed.

C. And it is there, a warm jewel in the womb of night. So
tiny, so vulnerable, so dependent, frailer than a cockle-
shell in the seas round Cape Horn. Dependent upon
the sun, dependent upon its atmosphere, dependent
upon its master and its own dependant, man.

D. And from out in infinite space we descend, down,
down, down to our own town (city/village); to one
district, one area, one building – this church.

(THE READINGS ARE FROM *FIELDS OF PRAISE* BY JOHN HARRIOTT.)

The minister asks individuals, 'How do you feel, after
those readings? Very small and insignificant; humbled and
of little worth? Whatever we feel, God loves and cares for
each one of us, made in his image and likeness.

HOLY SPIRIT: 'O HOLY SPIRIT, BREATHE ON ME' (*Mission Praise* 500)

This activity is particularly suitable for Pentecost. Give out
randomly to a variety of people (not just children) twelve
red balloons. Ask those with balloons to blow them up and
hold them. Comment: a balloon only becomes what it is
intended to be when it is filled with breath or air. Release
your balloons (have fun returning them to their owners):
now your red balloons look withered and spent. It is the
same with us. The breath of the Holy Spirit fills us with
life and makes us the type of people God intended us to

be. Without the Spirit we are like a withered balloon. Why red balloons? – red is the colour associated with the Holy Spirit and twelve for the twelve Apostles who were the first to receive the Spirit on the day of Pentecost. Now let us sing our hymn.

INDIVIDUAL DIGNITY: 'LORD, THE LIGHT OF YOUR LOVE IS SHINING' (*Mission Praise* 445)

This activity is suitable for Pentecost. Give out a number of candles randomly to a variety of people – the candles must all have different sizes, shapes and colours. Comment how each candle is different, and each person holding the candle is different: different ages, stages of life, etc. With this one flame (lit with a taper) I will come and light each candle. (Accompanying action.) Now all candles have the same size flame, regardless of the size, colour or shape of the candle.

It is exactly the same with us; the fire of the Holy Spirit comes to 'light us up' regardless of our age, our size, our place in society and career. The Spirit is the same for all. God is not interested in what age we are, what colour we are, what social class we belong to. He only wants us to be alight with his love and a living witness to the love of God. Now let us sing our hymn.

IN GOD'S HANDS: 'HE'S GOT THE WHOLE WORLD' (*Mission Praise* 225)

Place in full view a good sized globe of the world, then ask a child to come out and show everyone where the British

Isles is. Now ask an adult to come forward and point out Israel, or any other place. Ask the question, 'What was the name of the Greek god of mythology who was a Titan and was condemned to hold up the heavens or the globe?' The answer is Atlas. Make the link between the Greek god and a book, or the globe which shows the countries of the world. God is like Atlas. He holds up the world, he has the whole of the universe in his hand. Everything was, and is, made by Him. Sing the hymn.

JESUS OUR ALL: 'JESUS THE LORD'
(*Mission Praise* 384)

Five volunteers of all ages are asked to stand up where they are in the church (as long as they can be heard). If time permits it would be ideal for each to hold up a symbol of what they are saying, for example the first would have a loaf of bread, the second the road sign for One Way, the third a flash light, etc.

The first says: 'I want to thank God for bread, which stands for all the food we need in order to live.'

The second: 'I want to thank God for giving us faith, so that our lives have direction and purpose. We know where we are going.'

The third: 'I want to thank God for light, which represents the freedom we have to practise our Christian faith.'

The fourth: 'I want to thank God for the way he cares for us all, like a shepherd cares for his sheep.'

The fifth: 'I want to thank God for the gift of life that we enjoy and the promise of life with God forever.'

Following this the hymn is sung.

JESUS OUR SAVIOUR: 'BLESSED ASSURANCE' (*Mission Praise* 59)

Two or three popular newspapers, local or national, are needed. The minister draws attention to several human stories in the papers. He speaks of the insatiable curiosity that people have about others lives and affairs. Stories suited to youngsters as well as adults should be included.

He comments on the fact that everyone present has a story to tell, of hard times, of exciting events, of painful experiences, etc. While this is true, Christians are aware of their total dependence upon God and his loving providence. Our greatest story is of how Jesus has been our rescuer, our saviour, on so many occasions in life and as the Saviour of all humanity. The hymn is now sung.

JOY IN LIVING: 'REJOICE IN THE LORD ALWAYS' (*Mission Praise* 577)

This activity needs an adult or a child dressed as a clown, or a doll in clown's clothes. If there is a real clown who can appear just for a few moments, all the better. Now comment on clowning for God. There is an Anglican priest who is a professional clown and he is in great demand in leading workshops and worship. His book, *Fools Rush In*, shows how 'God chose the foolish things of this world to shame the wise'. There is a Holy Fools Association of Christian clowns in this country with more than 200 members.

'God is infinite fun' and wants us to be happy. Joy is one of the gifts of the Holy Spirit and a spirit of joy is possessed by all those who come close to God. Now let us sing our hymn.

LIVING FOR GOD: 'TAKE MY LIFE'
(*Mission Praise* 624)

This activity requires a house brick and a wide plank of wood or a sheet of plywood. The plank is positioned at a 45° angle, propped against a chair or table. The minister or speaker holds the brick in her/his hand and asks, 'What will happen if I place this brick at the top of this slide? Yes, it will slide down. (Match action to words.) Now as it is sliding down, is it easy to stop? No; possible, but not easy.

It is the same with our lives. We develop bad habits, laziness about our prayers, occasional lies and half-truths, etc. We slide, and it is not easy to stop. The only answer is to take a firm grip on ourselves (match words to action of firmly holding the brick) and every day resolve to offer ourselves and all that we are to God our Father, for he is the only one who can 'stop the brick'. Sing the hymn.

NAMES OF GOD: 'FATHER WE LOVE YOU'
(*Mission Praise* 142)

The children and young people need to prepare large sheets of paper or posters with a title of God written clearly in large print. Have as many as possible, 'The Lord', 'The Almighty', 'The All-Powerful', 'The All-Knowing', 'Creator', etc., but they must not include the title 'Father' or 'Abba'. At the invitation of the minister the posters are brought out one by one, and shown to everyone. The minister then asks the adults to tell which name is missing, after which the comment is made that the Islamic faith has ninety-nine names for God, but not one of them is 'Father', the title the Son of God himself gave us. Now the hymn can be sung.

POWER OF GOOD EXAMPLE: 'GIVE ME OIL IN MY LAMP' (*Mission Praise* 167)

Give out an assortment of batteries, of all sizes and shapes. Ask a child, 'What have I given to you?' Comment on use of batteries in flash cameras, transistors, etc. Ask adults for ideas on sources of power before batteries were invented (gas supply, oil lamps, etc.) Modern batteries in torches are the nearest equivalent to the hand-held oil lamps of the time of Jesus. As Christians our source of energy for good is God himself.

RESPECTING CREATION: 'ALL CREATURES OF OUR GOD AND KING' (*Mission Praise* 7)

A quantity of playdough needs to be prepared (recipe in appendix 1). The minister gives a small ball of it to each child and adult present. They are asked to make any animal or creature of their choice. While they are doing this the minister speaks of St Francis of Assisi and his love of nature.

He can then read the following, or the Canticle of the Sun of Francis.

The end was fast approaching. Two days before his death he asked to be stripped of all his clothes, and to be put on the ground that he might die in the arms of Lady Poverty.

It was on the night of October 3, 1226, that he

breathed his last, praising God to the end. With his songs were mingled those of the little birds he loved so well, for we are told that a great multitude of larks came above the roof of the house where he lay, and, flying a little way off, made a circle round the roof, and by their sweet singing seemed to be praising the Lord along with him.

(FROM AN ANCIENT SOURCE.)

The minister now goes round the children with the playdough and admires their creations, asking what they are. The minister reminds everyone that as the children have made their own animals, so God has made us and all creatures. We all owe praise to God.

The hymn is now sung.

RETURNING TO GOD: 'AMAZING GRACE'
(*Mission Praise* 31)

Before the service the minister hides something, like a familiar hymn book that he uses, somewhere in the church.

He tells the children that he has pretended to lose it so they can go and find it for him. While the children are away hunting for the object, the minister asks the adults to think about what happens and what they do when they lose their car keys or house keys. An individual might be encouraged to tell of such an occasion. When the children return the minister speaks about losing and finding things, how worried we get, the problems it causes, etc.

At this point the minister can read the story of Jesus about the lost coin (Luke 15:8–10) or the lost sheep (Luke 15:1–7), after which the hymn can be sung.

Spiritual Growth: 'Teach me to live, day by day' (*Mission Praise* 627)

Obtain a packet of seeds (beetroot is quite good for this) and put one in the palm of each person's hand. Comment: Paul says, 'Never grow weary of doing good' (Galatians 6:9). The seed you have in your hand is very small and it looks quite dead, but you know that if it is put into the ground, watered and kept warm it will grow. It will give out a shoot and grow into a plant. The Christian life is like that; it needs patience, it needs light and water and warmth. It needs nurturing or it will fail. Patience and perseverance will bring a harvest. Paul says, 'Let us not become weary in doing good, for at the proper time we will reap a harvest if we do not give up.' Now sing the hymn.

The Holy Name: 'I love the name of Jesus' (*Mission Praise* 285)

The minister holds up to view a teddy bear, or a doll, and speaks about the bear/doll's name. She/he then asks those present, adults as well as children, to confess if they have or once had a favourite teddy or doll. Comment: it is important to name a teddy or doll – or a pet – because the bond between you and the toy or pet is closer and more personal once a name is given. Names of people often mean something (give examples). The name 'Jesus' was quite common in New Testament time, that's why he was called Jesus of Nazareth, to distinguish him from other men of the same name. Our English 'Jesus' comes from the Hebrew *Yehosua*, or Joshua. It means 'God saves', so you could say the word 'Jesus' means 'saviour'; which of course he was for us. Sing the hymn.

THE LORD'S SUPPER: 'LET US BREAK BREAD TOGETHER' (*Mission Praise* 414)

This activity is suitable for a Eucharist or Communion Service which is also a church parade service. Have at hand one of the flags which has been presented at the commencement of the service and also the bread and the wine.

A guide or a scout is requested to bring the flag (from wherever the colours are placed) and in a loud voice say, 'This flag is a symbol of our company and of our loyalty to the Guide/Scout Movement. We take and try to keep the Guide/Scout promise.'

The minister replies, 'This bread, with this wine, is the symbol of our company or community, as Christians. Christ has made a promise to be always with us. This symbol reminds us of his promise to us and our promise to be faithful to him. Our God is a God of Promise and we are the people of that Promise.

The representative guide/scout then returns to his seat and the minister can enlarge upon the theme of being a company or community of Christians with the Eucharist at its centre, which sustains us spiritually as we try to live by the promise. Sing the hymn.

TRUST IN GOD: 'DO NOT BE AFRAID'
(*Mission Praise* 115)

The minister asks a young person in the congregation 'What frightens you?' (The answer might be 'spiders' or 'the dark', etc.) Ask several more children the same question. Then ask an adult, 'What is your first name? Do you know if it has a meaning?' (For example, Sarah means 'princess'.) Ask several other adults the same question.

Then comment: we have spoken of fears and personal names; now a short story. A little boy was afraid of the dark and asked to sleep in his parents' bedroom with them. He woke in the night and called out, 'Daddy.'

His father replied, 'What is it? Are you all right?'

The boy replied, 'Is your face towards me, Daddy?'

'Yes, Thomas,' the father replied.

'Good,' said the boy, 'now I know I'm all right.' And he went back to sleep.

'Is your face towards me?' God knows each of us personally by name; we can address him as 'Abba', Daddy, and whatever we fear, his face is turned towards us. His name and his presence dispel fear.

The singing of the hymn now takes place.

5

ALL-AGE LEARNING

JESUS THE TEACHER

Jesus was deeply involved in all-age learning. The groups and crowds that he spoke to were drawn from all sections of the community – the educated rabbis from Jerusalem and the fishermen of Galilee, the young and the old, women and men.

'Here is a boy with five loaves and two small fish' (John 6:9). There were certainly children present when Jesus taught the mixed crowds.

Jesus is referred to as 'teacher' forty-eight times in the New Testament and his work as 'teaching' fifty times; and yet nowadays we rarely think of him as a teacher.

What can we learn from Jesus, the all-age teacher? To begin with there is his obvious love of people; no teacher can be successful if she/he does not love, in the Christian sense, the 'students'. This means seeing them as subjects, not as objects. (But more of this below.)

Next there is the deep knowledge and appreciation that Christ had of the content of his teaching. It came from within, it had been thought about and lived for years before he started to share 'the Good News'. He did not refer to a written book, or sit behind a desk. Jesus had immediate contact with the people.

As we saw earlier, he used stories and events from every-day life; Christ's teaching was very deep but never abstract and removed from the practical realities of everyday life. He spoke in the day-to-day language of the market place, not in words shaped by philosophy and hundreds of years of theological speculation. There appeared to be no educational barrier between Jesus and his audience. A modern university education can be (but need not be) an obstacle in the communication of God's word to the majority of working class people who left school at sixteen, and never read a book.

Jesus involved his 'students' in the learning process. Most of the parables he told were not simple direct stories, they needed thinking about. People were required to tease out the meaning and apply it.

When questioned Jesus never replied with a simple answer. He always made the questioner work at the answer himself by answering the question that Jesus would reply with, thereby becoming involved in their own learning.

For example, 'Teacher,' he asked, 'what must I do to inherit eternal life?'

'What is written in the Law?' Jesus replied. 'How do you read it?' (Luke 10:25).

In short Jesus was a successful teacher because he cared for his 'pupils', spoke directly and simply to them, from the heart, and involved them in their own learning by parables and well-placed questions.

THE FAITH JOURNEY

The Christian faith is not a static adhesion to a list of beliefs and moral practices, it is a life-long journey – an adventurous journey that needs education and support at every stage.

Thomas Groome said: 'The very journey to maturity of faith itself demands a struggle and a certain wrestling.'

Readers who are familiar with the work of this Christian educationalist from Boston, USA, will recognise a reliance upon his writings in the following pages.

What we are talking about here, of course, is religious education, not in a school setting, or the home, but in the third point of the triangle, the parish or church community. We have spoken of the simple methods of Christ our Lord, but in our modern setting there is nothing sure or simple about religious education. As Dietrich Bonhoeffer said, it is an enterprise where there is no 'cheap grace'.

Practically we can look a little closer at all-age learning, or religious education for all in the local Christian community, under the following headings: The What, The Why, The Where, The How, The When, The Who.

Before any teaching event is attempted, there needs to be a short training course with the planning team to examine these six foundation stones of Christian education. A team of willing, hopefully enthusiastic ordinary Christians cannot be expected to put together and lead learning events if they are not clear about their aims and objectives.

The What

The 'what' for Jesus was 'the Kingdom of God'. All his parables and miracles illustrated and supported his teaching on the Kingdom of God. It was the central theme and purpose in the teaching and life of Jesus.

It can be no different for us. Our purpose is to promote a Christian faith that is lived in response to the Kingdom of God, in Jesus Christ. Individually, and collectively as a faith community, we are on a journey towards greater maturity in the Christian faith.

What, for example, do we understand by 'The Kingdom of God'? Considerable misunderstandings have arisen over Matthew's use of the alternative 'Kingdom of Heaven'. Modern Christians need to appreciate that he is not referring to a place, but, as an Orthodox Jew, he is using an alternative for the word 'God', which no good Jew would use.

It should not be taken for granted that all will share the same understanding of the word Faith.

The Apostle Paul is the New Testament exponent on faith. When discussing faith the starting point is: faith is a gift of God. 'It is by grace that you have been saved, through faith; not by anything of your own, but by a gift from God' (Ephesians 2:8).

'Although it is a gift if people are to come to a lived relationship with God, in Jesus Christ, then the faith story of the Christian Community must be encountered in lived experience' (Thomas Groome).

There are two dimensions to faith: it embraces belief and trust. Faith can be developed in the sense that one can learn more and more about the content of divine revelation, although not all 'beliefs' are of equal importance. This is the *cognitive dimension*. It can equally include the deepening of the faith of more mature members of the community or an attempt to show the reasonableness of Christian beliefs to those young in the faith.

Faith encompasses the activity of trust too. This is the *affective dimension*. So Christian faith is an invitation by God to a relationship of loyalty and trust.

Now faith, in both senses of belief and trust, demonstrates its presence and reality in action. 'What good is it, my brothers, if a man claims to have faith but has no deeds?... Faith by itself, if it is not accompanied by action, is dead' (James 2:14ff).

So there is a *behavioural dimension* to Christian faith, an activity of doing, of engagement in the world.

The purpose of all-age learning is necessarily the same as religious education, which is the promotion of a lived Christian faith through the three activities of believing, trusting and doing.

The Why

What is the consequence for 'pilgrims' on the Christian journey living such a life of Christian faith? It has to be a consequence related to the Kingdom; a making present of that Kingdom and a contribution to the Kingdom's final completion.

'I have come,' Jesus said, 'that they may have life, and have it to the full' (John 10:10).

'So if the Son sets you free, you will be free indeed' (John 8:36).

The consequence that we are talking about is human freedom. It is very useful to approach any discussion about human freedom under the headings, 'freedom for' and 'freedom from'.

Created in the image of God, we are a reflection of the free creator and so 'free for God', which liberates us to be 'free for ourselves' and 'free for others'. So 'freedom for' allows us to become the type of persons God intended.

An awareness of our dignity and the dignity of others brings us to an awareness of and a striving for 'freedom from' any kind of injustice or oppression.

The Where

The communal context of learning is an expression of one of the most fundamental principles of the Christian tradition, as we have already seen it is for worship. All-age learning is nothing new; it is the oldest and surest way of maturing in the Christian faith. It is within a people that we come to birth, grow and find salvation.

'They accepted what he (Peter) said and were baptized. That very day three thousand were added to their number. These remained faithful to the teaching of the Apostles, to the brotherhood, to the breaking of bread and to the prayers' (Acts 2:41).

So in providing all-age learning we are not chasing a new fashion but returning to our roots.

The How

In the church community learning is a together-experience; all are learners. The Christian story and vision are not imparted by those who have the mysteries to those who do not have them. In the whole all-age community the 'story' is not simply told, it is encountered in the lives of those who are living it. The Lord's own example can be seen in the Road to Emmaus story: 'As they talked and discussed these things with each other, Jesus himself came up and walked along with them' (Luke 24:15).

Jesus 'walked along with them': those who are more mature in the Faith walk along with those who are less mature, so that 'their eyes will be opened and they will recognise him' (v. 31).

The method of Joseph Cardijn, favoured by the Roman Catholic Church, comes to mind here, the principle of 'See, Judge and Act'. Together we see what there is to see and learn, for example in the story of the two disciples on the road to Emmaus. Then together we form a judgment on how it applies to our lives. We then act upon the knowledge. And we review that action together at the next meeting.

The When

The atmosphere in which all-age learning is conducted must be one of trust. The physical environment should be welcoming and encouraging in its warmth and openness. The 'when' for individuals varies from person to person. For example much research has shown that it is a waste of time to try to teach abstract concepts to small children. Only from about twelve years of age can a person begin to reflect critically. Up to that age all learning must be in concrete terms.

There must be a desire and willingness to learn in the community, for Christian learning should never be foisted upon any age group.

The Who

All are called to make a faith journey. The call, as recounted in the Parable of the Sower, may fall on deaf ears, or it may start growing and get choked or get stunted in other ways. All those who have already set out as pilgrims on the journey could be co-partners in learning. Thomas Groome points out that those who desire to lead other people along the road to Christian maturity need to be ever moving inward, to move outward with others. The 'students' of whatever age and social standing are brothers and sisters, fellow pilgrims and co-partners in the learning. From this follows the thought that all 'students' are subjects, never objects.

Students are not people to be made into 'good Anglicans' or 'good Methodists' or 'good Catholics', but rather people who are called to engage in the world to make present the Kingdom of God.

CREATING OPPORTUNITIES

All those who set out to provide all-age events should from time to time remind themselves of this text: 'Let us not become weary in doing good, for at the proper time we will reap a harvest if we do not give up' (Galatians 6:9).

Experienced readers will know that patience and perseverance are the two key virtues required of all those who want to engage in all-age learning activities.

Much effort can go into planning and preparation, accompanied by good advertising, and the response can be poor and disappointing. The very human and understandable reaction from the organisers can be, why bother? That would be a sad mistake; for while good numbers should be worked for and hoped for, an event is not worthless because only a small number respond. Remember that the shepherd, in Christ's parable, left the ninety-nine and went after the one lost sheep. There is more joy in heaven over good achieved with one person than over ninety-nine who do not need it.

Jesus, too, was not always 'successful'. He started with twelve close friends, but one betrayed him and one denied even knowing him. There was a harvest though, for from the eleven who survived the passion and death of Jesus there grew the 1.5 billion Christians who are in the world today.

It is true too that some are called by God to prepare the ground, some to sow the seed, and others to reap and harvest what was sown. Each in God's plan has a role to play. In community activities it is often the case that others, in the future, may reap (and perhaps even claim credit) from our present hard work.

These are thoughts that the All-Age Activities (Learning) Team leader needs to share with his team.

Our task is to provide opportunities for the members of our community, not to seek success, measured by numbers, in the here and now.

Those opportunities may be taken up or they may not, for no organiser can ever be certain of encouraging numbers. But she or he can be certain that God needs us to present opportunities to his people and he will use those opportunities, if only to reach one or two.

The local community needs to become 'learning-conscious', in other words, aware of the need to seize ordinary simple opportunities as occasions for instruction, encouragement and growth. For example, an older woman or man, or a couple, may be engaged in some activity in the church or its surroundings, a number of youngsters may stop to talk to them, and suddenly an opportunity has been presented for the more mature Christians to explain what they are doing and why.

Deliberately planned opportunities include the following:

Half an hour after the Sunday service – this is only any good if it is tightly planned, to start and end promptly, making full use of the thirty minutes.

Half a day – a two/three hour session filling a morning or an afternoon is very popular with families because in family life there are always many things that require time. It is also easier on catering arrangements than a full day.

A day-long workshop – one of the most satisfying events for all age groups.

An evening session – not popular with families, unless early evening and including simple catering arrangements.

An outing – a visit to a cathedral, historical Christian site, shrine etc. These are very popular with elderly people and youngsters.

An all-night vigil – popular with teengers and some of the middle-aged; not suitable for children under twelve or the elderly.

A weekend away – popular with middle-class families, particularly if there is a leisure dimension and plans include the very young.

These suggestions do not exhaust the possibilities but may stimulate other ideas to meet a particular community's needs.

If an event is successful the organising team should 'trumpet' that success widely. This will encourage the timid and cautious to take part next time. People like to be associated with successful ventures.

PRACTICAL PLANNING POINTS

Much of what was said in chapter 1 about planning for all-age worship applies equally to the learning context.

It is important to form a team – this is even more import-ant with learning than with worship. Most communities have members who are professional teachers, both primary and secondary (take care to include both because different teaching styles are involved and, of course, age groups). These should be approached and invited to be 'advisers'. Many full-time teachers do not wish to teach at weekends (it's too much like work). This should be respected and appreciated, but if they are committed Christians many would be prepared to advise a group of enthusiastic parishioners. And of course once they get involved in the life of the team these teachers might offer a little more than advice.

Once the planning team has been composed the members need a number of training or preparatory sessions together. A consideration of the issues raised in this section, or something similar, could form the basis of such training. It is imperative that the organising team start with the same vision and shared purpose, otherwise much time will be wasted at planning meetings with sincere people in conflict.

It is advisable to restrain the over-enthusiastic who are likely to propose an ambitious plan for the coming year. The team would do well to remember the parable of the mustard seed and the saying 'great oaks from little acorns grow'. Moderate success with a modest venture can develop gradually into more ambitious projects. This will build the confidence of the team and the church community, and whet people's appetite for a full day or a weekend event.

The key word in planning and executing a learning experience is involvement. The participants, of whatever age or background, must be involved in their own learning and there must be no passive participants. The planners must keep that principle before them, whatever type of opportunity is to be offered to the community. In practice this means that arranging a speaker, as one might do for the Women's Fellowship, will not be suitable unless the speaker is going to do much more than speak. At the very least she or he would need to speak *with* not *to* the gathered group (and what of the children?) engaging them in a 'conversation' rather than a passive audience role.

In the following practical suggestions, which are offered more as guides than outlines to be followed without localising them, the emphasis is entirely upon active participation by everyone present at the learning event. Making, drawing, painting, acting, discussing, writing, singing, etc. must be used to the full. No action is too simple or too difficult not to be tried.

CHOOSING TOPICS

The long-term aim of the planning team is to help the community deepen their knowledge, understanding and appreciation of the central doctrines of the Christian Church.

However it would be a little unwise to start with the Holy Trinity or Redemption. It would be better to start with an easier topic like 'Discipleship' or 'The Meaning of Love' (see chapter 3) and graduate to more difficult topics as the experience of the team grows.

Some of the best topics arise out of the life and interests of the community. For example, the Anglican church on Abbey Wood estate, South London, is called The William Temple Church. A good starting topic there would be, 'Who was William Temple?' He was, of course, a remarkable Archbishop of Canterbury in the 1940s.

At an all-age learning experience a huge collage (or two) could be put together for hanging in the church. The youngsters can be guided to produce a map showing where Canterbury is, with pictures of Canterbury Cathedral, etc. Teenagers could research other famous archbishops, and perhaps illustrate what happened to Thomas Becket. The middle-aged participants could learn a little about William Temple's social teaching and apply it to the social questions of today. Others might like to find pictures illustrating the Second World War and mount them alongside the text of William Temple's proposal for a post-war Britain. Older members would need to help the youngsters find and present the material and all could have a fun-time deciding on the design and execution of the collage.

Once there is a degree of experience the planning group should look seriously at the topics referred to earlier in this chapter: Faith, the Kingdom of God, the parables of Jesus.

The planning team must never be over-anxious about tackling the more substantial topics. It is not 'putting on' events for people, but offering occasions when all, team and participants, learn together.

AFTER THE EVENT

It requires energy and not a little humility to arrange a review of the event shortly afterwards. This should not be on the same day but about a week later, in order to allow people time to reflect on how it went. It would be wise to make this an established practice, so that there is a constant effort to learn and improve.

It requires humility to ask for participants' honest evaluation of the event. Ask questions like, Was it too long? Did everyone present feel that they were welcome and involved? Did the event achieve its objective? All the team can ask for the sincere views of those, of all ages, who took part and carry these back to the review meeting. The comments of the young should be accorded the same serious consideration as everyone else.

For major events, like a whole day or weekend, an appraisal-of-the-day sheet could be prepared seeking the same information. This could be completed by everyone present as the last or last-but-one item on the programme.

Those in the community who have not taken part can still learn, indirectly, from the event. Exhibition display boards are not cheap but they are well worth investing in and can give years of service. Strategically placed at the back of the church, the 'work' of the event-participants can be displayed for all to see. This not only informs the church members who did not attend, it also demonstrates what happens at such an event and advertises the next one.

Take care, however, not to leave the display up for too long. It should be removed after two or three weeks, before it loses its freshness and becomes tatty and soiled.

6

SAMPLES OF ALL-AGE LEARNING

The ideas outlined in this section are simply samples, with the emphasis upon variety. The ideas given will prompt fuller and more appropriate plans to suit an individual community.

SIGNIFICANT PEOPLE

REQUIREMENTS

Lined and plain paper, pencils and pens.
An elderly, respected member of the community who is prepared to speak for a few minutes on 'How important Jesus is for me'.

All those present are asked to take a piece of lined paper and, if they wish, a piece of plain paper, and go to a quiet corner of the room or hall and either write about or draw a picture of any person who has been important or significant in their lives. (The children may need assistance; they will, almost certainly, draw a picture of mum or dad, or both.) If they have time they could write a little prayer for their significant person. This should only take a maximum of ten minutes.

All return together. Everyone is invited (no one is compelled) to show everyone else their picture and explain who it is and why that person is significant for them, or to read out what they have written.

When this has been completed the elderly member of the community explains simply 'How important Jesus is for me'. This short session can conclude with a time of prayer, praying aloud the prayers that have been written. The session leader can bring it to a conclusion with a prayer thanking God for Jesus.

WHAT CAME FIRST?

Dinosaurs or Adam and Eve – what came first?

REQUIREMENTS

A good book from the local library on the ages of the earth and the development of life on the planet.
Three lengths of wallpaper (blank side to be used), about two metres long.
Pencils, colouring pens, glue, A4 white paper.
Three group leaders.

PREPARATORY WORK

All the children and young people who are going to attend are invited to bring 'a dinosaur' and be ready, if they wish, to tell others about it. Adults are invited to bring their Bibles.

Divide those present into three mixed groups and give each its own working space or area. Each receives a length of wallpaper and a selection of writing and colouring pens.

The group leaders encourage the young people to show the group their dinosaurs and tell everyone what type it is and, if possible, when it roamed the planet. Each group then gets to work on its own project.

Group One uses the reference book on the ages of the earth and shares out tasks. The wallpaper is divided lengthways into the principal ages from Pre-Cambrian to Holocene (including the Jurassic period and the age of the dinosaurs). The young people locate where their dinosuars fit in and each period is illustrated. Much adult help will be required. (Many adults will learn about dinosaurs from the youngsters.)

Group Two reads together the first story of creation in the Bible (Genesis 1:1–31 and 2:1–3). It then divides the length of wallpaper (lengthways) into seven sections representing the seven days. These are identified and illustrated according to what God created on each day. The seventh day could have a cartoon picture of 'God resting', or just the words The Sabbath, Day of Rest, with pictures of the things we do on Sundays.

Group Three reads together the second story of creation in the Bible (Genesis 2:4–25). The group will need to discuss how they are going to divide up their strip of wallpaper lengthways.

When the groups have their displays ready (or when time runs out) they gather together again and the three lengths are displayed, one above the other on an empty wall. The dinosaur sheet can go at the top, then the first story of the creation and under that the second story.

The session leader now asks questions to draw out the lesson that there are two Bible accounts of creation, and they cannot both be accurate. The group can see, from the displays, that the accounts are quite different; they teach different messages because that is what they are, teaching stories, rather like parables. They convey not scientific fact but religious teaching, that there is one God who is a mighty creator, etc. The Bible stories do not set out to tell us the scientific *how*, but the religious *why* of creation. Other interesting lessons may be drawn, but care must be taken to do no more than answer the question, 'What came first, dinosaurs or Adam and Eve?' Adults may like to continue the discussion another time.

DISCIPLESHIP

REQUIREMENTS

An assortment of pens, pencils, colouring felt tips, crayons etc. (The team needs to build up a store of such vital materials.)
Plain A4 sheets of paper and rolls of redundant wallpaper.

The all-age gathering is divided into two groups, with the ages mixed. They are told the theme and that each group will have the name of one disciple of Jesus given to them. They are to keep the name secret from the other group.
The groups separate to different rooms or areas and prepare a presentation on their apostle – one is given the name Simon Peter and the other Judas. Using the Bible and with the aid of a list of useful references, they may use any means they like – a collage, a poster, a play, etc – to show what sort of follower their named person was, with strengths and weaknesses, faults and failings.

Each group will be invited back to make a presentation to the other group. (Who goes first can be decided by the toss of a coin.) While accurate information must be given, the name of the disciple must not be used, because the other group will be timed to see how long it is before they accurately guess the correct name. To avoid random names being called out, there is a two-minute penalty on each inaccurate name suggested. (Naturally there has to be an agreed referee and score keeper.)

After each presentation has been made – and a winner declared – with the aid of a blackboard, whiteboard or large sheet of paper, compare the two Apostles, like this:

Peter:		*Judas:*	
	Chosen by Jesus		Chosen by Jesus
	Trusted by Jesus		Trusted by Jesus
	Travelled with Jesus		Travelled with Jesus
	Denied knowing Jesus		Betrayed Jesus
	Ashamed of his action		Ashamed of his action
	Hoped for forgiveness		Despaired of forgiveness
	Told Jesus he loved him		Killed himself in despair

What lessons are there for each of us, no matter what age we are, as we try to be the followers of Jesus?

MORAL TALES

REQUIREMENTS

A supply of paper and writing materials.
Several Ladybird books.

With this activity adults must be reassured that although children's traditional stories are being used, there is a real value in being involved.

The number of stories used will depend upon the number of mixed groups of six people that can be made up, with different ages and genders. Each group needs one book. The Ladybird versions are standard in presentation and very easily obtainable – most families have copies which they will be happy to loan. Use stories like *The Enormous Turnip, Chicken Licken, The Princess and the Frog, The Golden Goose, The Three Little Pigs, The Gingerbread Man, Beauty and the Beast*.

All of them have a clear moral to the story. For example, *The Enormous Turnip* makes it clear that if all in a community, the greatest and the smallest, work together even a huge task can be achieved. In *Chicken Licken* the moral is, do not blindingly follow a leader, without thought and question. (Very appropriate for teenagers who follow peers without question.)

The groups of six are given a book each (it is best not to let the groups choose) and sent off to their own venues, to read the story and work out the moral together. Each group then prepares is own dramatised version and thinks of a fresh way to convey the moral of the tale to the other groups. The group can also try to think of an incident in the life of Jesus, or one of his parables, that echoes or connects with the moral of the story.

There can be great fun when the plays are shared. With good leadership keeping it all together, it can be a very beneficial experience for all participants. Besides the content of the topic, shared events like this offer growth in a sense of community.

GET TO KNOW YOUR BIBLE

REQUIREMENTS

Enough Bibles for one between two people.
Booklets of questions are available, free of charge, from Gideons International. (Write to Gideons International, Western House, George St, Lutterworth, Leics., LE17 4EE.) These have been supplied free of charge to schools and are excellent for all age groups to use.

The Bibles are distributed to pairs of people, where possible older more experienced church members with younger ones. A simple introduction is necessary along the lines of 'Let's now look at our Bibles and find where the Gospels are'.

Then the gathering splits into pairs to work on the booklets. It might be a good idea to provide simple prizes, like bookmarks, for those who finish first, or in a given time.

BIBLE CHARACTERS: NAME BINGO

REQUIREMENTS

Two or three enthusiastic people who will spend time
making the game, as instructed below.

This is a kind of Name Bingo activity to involve all ages
following a theme on 'Names' or 'Persons in the Bible'.
Quite a lot of preparation is necessary for this game, but
once it has been made it can be played again and again in
the future.

1. Write down a list of Old Testament names, at least 30.
   (The NIV Study Bible has a subject list at the back which
   is invaluable.)
2. On an A5 sheet of paper, rule sixteen squares (four
   across, four down).
3. Randomly write three different names in three squares
   on line one, then repeat with other names for the
   remaining lines, making twelve names in total.
4. Repeat the last two steps on more sheets of paper (at
   least one for each person who will take part). Each
   sheet must be different.
5. Now make another set of names, and another set of
   papers divided into boxes, with New Testament names.
6. Copy all the names onto small cards, one name per
   card.

This is how the game is played:

1. Give each player a squared Old Testament and a New
   Testament sheet. Also give them 24 counters each. (You

could use pencils to mark the squares, but that would make the sheets unusable another time.)

2. Place all the small cards face down. The caller picks up a card and calls out the name written on it.

3. Players with a square containing that name place a counter on it.

4. The first person to get a completed line, that is, three covered names, wins the first small prize. Then the game can continue for four lines or full 'house'.

EASTER SYMBOLS

REQUIREMENTS

The 'symbols' listed below.
Separate areas where the groups can meet.
Writing, drawing and colouring materials for each group.

The gathering is divided into six mixed-age groups, with no more than six to a group. If necessary repeat several of the groups, as necessary.

The session leader may give a short introduction outlining our need for symbols and signs, and perhaps a comment that Easter bunnies occupy no place in Christian symbolism.

The groups are directed to separate areas and on arrival each is given an Easter symbol – a picture or, if possible, the real thing.

Group One receives an Easter or Paschal candle (it can be a used one from a previous year).

Group Two is loaned an Easter egg.

Group Three is given a hot-cross bun.

Group Four receives a picture of a lamb (or a cuddly knitted one)

Group Five is given a picture of an empty tomb.

Group Six gets a picture of a butterfly.

The groups are to discuss the meaning of their symbol. The adults agree upon the wording of a written presentation (including as much historical and background information as they can gather) while the youngsters can prepare a poster showing the symbol (which will be left behind in the group area when the group returns to the general gathering) with a few accompanying words.

After about half an hour the groups re-assemble, and then in turn make a presentation of their poster and their written work. Care must be taken to involve the younger members in this part of the activity.

THE EASTER WALK

REQUIREMENTS

None.

This can be used as part of any Eastertime learning activity. Based upon the story in Luke 24:13–35, the action recital is fun for all ages. All should stand, with the leader in full view.

The leader says the words below and everyone repeats them	*At the same time the leader shows the action, which all copy.*
Two friends of Jesus	holds up index finger of each hand

were walking to Emmaus. — walk on the spot
They were talking to one another — talking gesture with left hand
about all that had happened. — move right arm from side to side
While they were talking — talking gesture with left hand

Jesus joined them, — walk on spot
but they did not recognise him. — shake head, no sign
Jesus said to them, — talking gesture with hand
'What are you talking about?' — hold palms outstretched and half-extended
They told of Jesus's death on the cross — make a cross with two fingers
and how three days later — hold up three fingers
women found the tomb empty. — shrug shoulders

Jesus said to the two, — talking gesture
'How slow you are to believe — hand on heart
what the scriptures say.' — open hands like a book
The disciples asked Jesus to stay — summoning action with hand
and eat with them. — action of eating
At supper Jesus took the bread, — hold out right hand
blessed it and broke it. — two hands break bread
Then they recognised him, — take hand over eyes away
but Jesus had disappeared. — look around
The disciples hurried back to Jerusalem — walk quickly on spot

and told the apostles	talking gesture
all they had seen.	right finger points to eyes
How they recognised Jesus	take hands over eyes away
at the breaking of the	two hands break bread
bread.	

An Easter Trial

This could take place at any time of the year.

Requirements

A large room or hall set out, to suggest a courtroom.
For example, a judge's raised chair (dignified, perhaps
from the church); two rows of benches for the jury; a
'boxed' area for the witness stand, etc.

Volunteers to take the key parts; others to be members
of the jury, who only have to listen and vote. (If there
are too many for the jury, then there can be a public
gallery, if too few, spread the number over the jury
benches.)

Preparation

The characters, Mary Magdalene, Simon Peter, John, Mary,
mother of James and Salome, the guards, Mark, the evangelist (who is in the dock) etc. are given several days to
read Mark 15:33–47 and 16:1–20. They have to think
themselves into the part and read between the lines of the
Gospel so as to present a rounded character in court.

A distinguished judge is required and clerks of the
court. Parts must be found for the young people, eg.

Salome can be a young girl; and some of the boys can be the guards.

John Mark is in the dock and there is a prosecutor who calls witnesses to attest, on oath, that they really did find the tomb empty, etc.

Before the trial begins everyone must be told that all actors can develop their character's story as much as they like as long as they do not deviate from the basic story as told by Mark.

The charge before the court, read by the clerk of the court, is: 'That the accused, John Mark, formerly a resident of Jersualem, has deceived the Human Race by his fraudulent account that the tomb of Jesus of Nazreth, a convicted criminal, was empty and that he appeared alive to a group of his friends.'

The judge needs to have a thorough understanding of the Gospel text and gently give directions to the court, if necessary.

If time permits it is worthwhile to have a review session afterwards.

THE MEANING OF LOVE

REQUIREMENTS

Large sheets of white paper (one for each of the groups to make a poster).
Large felt-tipped colouring pens.
Six areas for the groups to work in. The groups are numbered one to six.

The gathering is divided into six equal groups of adults

and young people. A large sheet of paper for a poster and colouring pens are given to each group, and each has an appointed leader.

The groups go to their areas and only then are they told that each has a letter: 1 – C, 2 – A, 3 – R, 4 – I, 5 – N, 6 – G. This letter is to be drawn, as large as possible, on one side of the sheet of paper. (The group keeps its letter secret from the other groups.)

The group leader now leads a short discussion on 'What is love?' The young people's ideas should be taken note of, as well as the adults. After about ten minutes the leader tells the group that they have to think up a completion to the caption, 'Love is...' After talking it over the group may decide that 'Love is belonging to a family' or 'Love is putting others first', etc. The group should agree together and not blindly accept the first idea proposed.

The completed caption is now copied on to the other side of the sheet of paper. The caption can then be decorated. The leader must ensure that this is a group activity involving all ages.

The completed poster is kept a secret from the other groups. One of the group, not the leader, is deputed to show the poster off at the appropriate time.

All groups are recalled and the leader calls out the poster-bearers to sit or stand in a line, in numerical order from left to right (so that the hidden word CARING is spelt out when the posters are reversed.)

Each poster-bearer shows the Love is ... side to the whole gathering and reads out the caption. Each remains standing with the letter still hidden. Only when all six posters have been displayed does the leader say a word about the love that Jesus asks from us all. Not a romantic love, or even a friendship love, but a caring which should embrace everyone (Paul's description of love in 1 Corinthians 13:4–7 could be read here, or 1 John 4:7–21.) Then at a signal all the posters are turned round to reveal the word CARING.

CAPERNAUM

REQUIREMENTS

Sufficient copies of Peter's house (see below) for each group to have two or three each. Young artists may be encouraged, some days before, to copy the drawing and have it enlarged on a photocopier.

Maps of Israel, one for each group. The Israeli Tourist Board, with an office in London, will be happy to supply copies.

OPENING NOTE

Jesus was born in Bethlehem and brought up in Nazareth, but at the opening of his ministry he was driven out of his home town and he made Capernaum his new home and the centre of his ministry. At the site of that lakeside town modern archaeologists have identified and excavated the family home of Peter, where Jesus is believed to have lived with the family. The artist's impression below is based upon the discoveries at the site; it is as authentic a picture of the excavated house as the specialists can get it. (The house stands only some fifty yards from the lakeside.)

When assembled the gathering needs to be divided into all-age groups of six to eight people. These groups, in turn, are divided into two; the older members and the younger.

View of Peter's house at the time of Jesus

A picture of the house is given to each sub-group to work
on separately.

The group of older folk is asked to look at the picture
and decide which part of the house would have housed
Peter and his wife and family; which would have been the
part lived in by Peter's mother-in-law; which room would
possibly be used by Jesus; and what the remaining rooms,
areas and spaces would be used for.

After discussion and mutual agreement, the picture can
be marked and on the reverse reasons given for the choice.
Next, using the map of Israel, the sub-group must decide
why Jesus chose to live in this particular town, listing the
advantages and disadvantages from the point of view of his
ministry.

Meanwhile the young people (provided they are old
enough) separately answer the same questions.

After sufficient time each group re-assembles and the
two sub-sections of each group compare notes. When some
measure of common agreement is reached the group is
ready to report back to the general gathering.

North Meets South

Requirements

Two large separate rooms or halls and two leaders who
have been prepared.
A 'scribe' for each group with writing materials.
Two white free-standing boards for the presentation.

Divide the gathering into two groups of equal size, with
equal distribution of ages in each. One is 'The North' and
the other is 'The South'. They are situated in two separate

places so that neither can see what the other is preparing. Each group will need a leader and a scribe to record and report back.

'The North' group is told that all the members live in Britain, a European country, North America or Australia. (This information should only be given when the group has separated from 'The South'. They are to make a comprehensive list of the electrical goods, eg. colour TV, stereo units, computer, dishwasher, that each family has. (Include the number where there are several TVs, video recorders, etc.) The leader of this group can encourage the subtle competitive spirit which will become evident: 'We have four TVs'; 'Well, we've got one in every room', etc. The children and young people must be involved and each encouraged to complete the statement, 'I could not live without ....' (Answers are likely to include the TV, stereo unit.)

'The South' group is told that their members live in Asia, Africa, South America or any Third World country in the Southern Hemisphere. They are to make a list of the possessions which they are likely to have, eg. a hut, a bowl, a spoon, one change of clothes. The children and young people are encouraged to pretend that they live in such a society and complete the statement, 'I could not live without ....'

When the two groups are reunited, after twenty minutes or so, 'The North' are invited to present their findings first (the impact is lost if 'The South' go first). If possible the presentation should be graphic and visual, listing items and numbers on a black or white board.

The second group then make their presentation on the other board, standing alongside the first. (The leader will, of course, point out that the people of The South have no electrical supply or water in their homes.)

The conclusion will be self-evident. We who live in the Northern Hemisphere are very rich compared to those who live in the South.

This activity can be followed by a) a service which reminds of Christ's words of warning to the rich and Matthew 19:16–26 and 25:31–46; b) a further activity to explore why there is such a huge gap between rich and poor; c) plans to twin with a poor community abroad to raise funds for Christian Aid, Cafod, etc.

Other ideas can be found in the excellent *It's Not Fair: A Handbook on World Development for Youth Groups* (Christian Aid/CAFOD).

THE COLOURFUL WORLD OF THE NEW TESTAMENT

REQUIREMENTS

This activity is suitable for a full day event.

Library books.
Craft materials (see below).

The Bible was written in a culture and land vastly different from our own. It is essential, therefore, that we understand the life-styles, manners and customs of that time if we are going to fully understand Scripture. The following can be adapted to the time available, filling an hour or more usefully a half or whole day. The more time given to it, the more the whole community will benefit, because the aim would be to mount an exhibition afterwards in the church, for all to see and learn from.

In preparation a member of the planning team should

visit the local library (central or main branch) and explain the project. Most libraries run a topic book loan scheme whereby they will collect together for you a whole range of books on the subject, suitable for all ages. (There are many excellent books currently available, including those published by Lion, Usborne, Bodley Head, etc.)

The all-age gathering needs to be divided into three equal groups. They will be 'The Romans', 'The Greeks' and 'The Jews'. In the opening session the leader points out that Jesus lived in a society that was influenced by three cultures – Greek, Roman and Aramaic (or Jewish). Jesus would have spoken some Greek, Hebrew and Aramaic; the Romans occupied this country and Greek amphitheatres and culture were everywhere.

Each group leader will need a little preparation before the day, in conjunction with the other two, to discuss and agree the topics to be explored. These should include housing, food, religion, etc. Each group is sent away to explore the same topics, using the books provided for their research. The children and young people can be fully employed copying pictures from the books, making arte-facts in clay, card, leather, etc.

It can be a very exciting and most productive day for all involved. Time should be allowed for each group to show off their achievements to the other two, and to mount the display for the church.

LIVING A COMMUNITY LIFE

This is a suggestion for a full day activity. It is advisable to produce a programme well before the event so that people, especially busy parents, can make plans to attend. The timetable should be strictly adhered to and even if events do not flow as intended for the day, the lunch break and the departure time should be adhered to. People will not support further days if they cannot rely upon the times advertised.

AIM

It is important to have a clear purpose for an event which involves a whole or a part of a day. The objective for this event is twofold: to help all participants to have a better insight, according to their degree of maturity, into the life of Religious Sisters; and to appreciate that a relevant form of worship is at the centre of every Christian community.

REQUIREMENTS

A leader for the day who has already viewed the video and made appropriate notes, bearing in mind the aim of the day. From the list of participants who have enrolled for the day make up two equal-sixed, mixed groups. (If there are fewer than sixteen, adapt the programme for one group.)
The video *Sister Act*, with permission to use it, if necessary.
A religious sister, either Roman Catholic or Anglican, as a guest speaker. (Seek the advice of a local R.C. or Anglican priest.)

The idea of the day is to show everyone the video, *Sister Act*, then explore in two separate groups the questions: a) does the film realistically show religious life as lived today? b) could the worship of our own community be enlivened?

Programme for the day:

10.00am	Welcome and introduction.
10.10am	Watch the video together.
11.40am	Break for refreshments.
11.50am	Group work A.
12.30pm	Lunch break.
1.30pm	Group work B.
2.10pm	General assembly: question time.
2.45pm	Prepare for Act of Worship.
3.15pm	Act of Worship.
3.45pm	Appraisal sheets completed.
4.00pm	Departure.

NOTES

Introduction: The leader should very simply explain what the day will cover and explore. The guest speaker should be introduced and everyone invited to talk to her during the breaks.

Video: Make sure that everyone, little and large, old and young, can see.

Refreshment break: Breaks should be 'elastic', that is, they can be extended or shortened to keep the programme on time.

Group work A: The first group stays with the Sister and discusses the film and the realities of religious life. The second group goes to a separate place to talk about the music and the question of lively music in our community.

Lunch break: Can be shortened if desirable.

Group work B: As for A, swapping the groups.

General assembly: This can easily be omitted, but everyone might like to know what has gone on in the other group, and there may be more questions for the guest speaker.

Prepare for Act of Worship: An opportunity for practical work for the youngsters especially. The leader should have some outline already prepared with ideas for involving everyone as much as possible.

Act of Worship: This follows from what has taken place, and need not involve a member of the clergy.

Appraisal sheets: A sheet already prepared requiring participants to tick boxes showing what they liked or disliked, and with space for suggestions for improvements.

Departure: A cup of tea might be provided before participants leave.

The planning team should collate the information from the completed appraisal sheets and make it available on the following Sunday.

APPENDIX 1 RESOURCES FOR ALL-AGE EVENTS AND WORSHIP

Every worthwhile activity needs resources: fortunately there is an abundance of material for all-age worship and events, and the list is growing constantly. Here is a varied selection of resources available in or through most Christian bookshops.

Music

Mission Praise – Combined edition (Marshall Pickering))
Let's Praise (Marshall Pickering)
Come and Praise (1 and 2) (BBC)
Partners in Praise (Galliard)
Faith Looking Forward (Oxford University Press)
Praising a Mystery (Wild Goose Publications)
Heaven Shall Not Wait (Wild Goose Publications)
Enemy of Apathy (Wild Goose Publications)
Love From Below (Wild Goose Publications)
Five Instant Glorias and a Creed (Kevin Mayhew Ltd)
Songs of the Spirit (1, 2 and 3) (Kevin Mayhew Ltd)
Hymns Old and New (Kevin Mayhew Ltd)
Celebration Hymnal (1 and 2) (Mayhew-McCrimmom Ltd)

Psalms For Today (CPAS/Jubilate Hymns)
Songs and Hymns of Fellowship – Vols 1–4 and Combined edition (Scripture Union)

Liturgical Resource Books

Patterns for Worship (The Liturgical Commission, Church House Publishing)
The Promise of His Glory (The Liturgical Commission, Church House Publishing)
Lent, Holy Week, Easter (The Liturgical Commission, Church House Publishing)
Enriching the Christian Year (compiled by Michael Perham, SPCK/Alcuin Club)
Springboard to Worship (Susan Sayers, Kevin Mayhew Ltd)
Including Children (Some overlap with the above – Susan Sayers, Kevin Mayhew Ltd)
Church Family Worship (Hodder & Stoughton)
Waiting for the Risen Christ (SPCK)

Prayer

A Treasury of Prayer (compiled by Tony Castle, Hodder & Stoughton)
Intercessions for the Church Year (Susan Sayers, Kevin Mayhew Ltd)
Prayers for Teenagers (Nick Aiken, Marshall Pickering)
Praying for People (compiled by Margaret Pawley, Triangle, SPCK)
Prayers for All Seasons (Beryl Bye, Lutterworth Press)
Lion Book Of Prayers (Lion Books)
Bread for Tomorrow (Janet Morley, SPCK/Christian Aid)

Teaching Children to Pray (Ruth Cardwell, Grail Publication)

Readings

The Dramatized Bible (Edited by M. Perry, Marshall Pickering)
The Columba Lectionary (Columba Press)
New World: The Heart of the New Testament in Plain English (Alan Dale, Oxford University Press)
Winding Quest: The Heart of the Old Testament in Plain English (Alan Dale, Oxford University Press)
Celebrating the Seasons of Life (compiled by Mary Batchelor, Lion Books)

Sermon Aids

Quotations for All Occasions (compiled by Tony Castle, Marshall Pickering)
Quotes and Anecdotes for Preachers and Teachers (Revised Edition, compiled by Tony Castle, Kevin Mayhew Ltd)
More Quotes and Anecdotes (compiled by Tony Castle, Fowler Wright Press)

Useful Collections

Pick and Mix (edited by Margaret Dean, NS/Church House Publishing)
Themes for Family Worship (Tony Castle, Marshall Pickering)
Assembly Praise (Tony Castle, Marshall Pickering)
Teaching the Bible to Children (Tony Castle, Marshall Pickering)

All Age Worship: A Collection of Ideas from the Diocese of Newcastle (compiled by the Rev. C. Clinch and Judith Sadler, Diocese of Newcastle)

It's Not Fair: A Handbook on World Development for Youth Groups (Christian Aid/CAFOD)

Children Celebrate (Joan Chapman, Marshall Pickering)

Drama

Act Justly (CAFOD and Christian Aid)

Fast Food (Paul McCusker, Monarch Publications)

Clearing Away the Rubbish (Adrian Plass, Monarch Publications)

Eh, Jesus... Yes Peter... ? (Vol 1, 2, 3, John Bell and Graham Moule, Wild Goose Publications)

Drama for Disciples (Derek Haylock, NS/Church House Publishing)

Sketches from Scripture (Derek Haylock, NS/Church House Publishing)

Show Me 1, Creative Resources 1 (Bible Society)

Footnotes (Steve and Janet Stickley, Hodder & Stoughton)

Puppets in Praise (Stuart Holt, Marshall Pickering)

Background Reading/General Resources

Together Anthologies (Material from the magazine Together, NS/Church House Publishing. Together Magazine details from The National Society, Church House, Great Smith St, London SW1P 3NZ)

All Age Worship (Maggie Durran, Angel Press)

Children in the Way (Report from General Synod Board of Education, NS/Church House Publishing)

Liturgy and Liberty (John Leach, MARC Publishing)
Know How To Encourage Family Worship (Howard Mellor, Scripture Union)
Storytelling: Imagination and Faith (William Bausch, Twenty-Third Publications)
Gateway to the Trinity (Tony Castle, St Paul Publications)

Posters and Prints

An excellent range of liturgical posters, designed and executed by Turvey Abbey, is available from St Paul Multi-Media Productions. The series for Advent and Lent are recommended. These are available from any of the four St Paul Book Centres:

St Paul Book Centre, 133 Corporation St, Birmingham B4 6PH. Tel: 021 236 1619.

St Paul Book Centre, 5A Royal Exchange Square, Glasgow, G1 3AH. Tel: 041 226 3391.

St Paul Book Centre, 82 Bold St, Liverpool L1 4HR. Tel: 051 709 1328.

St Paul Book Centre, 199 Kensington High St, London W8 6BA. Tel: 071 937 9591.

Recipe for Playdough

This is used for making animal models in chapter 4.

2 cups of plain flour
2 cups of water
(colouring can be added to the water)
2 tablespoons of cooking oil
2 teaspoons of cream of tartar

1 cup of salt

Mix and cook on a low heat for about ten minutes or until the mixture thickens. Remove from heat and knead like dough.

Store the playdough in a sealed container – it does not need to be kept in the fridge.

Appendix 2 Clip Art for All-Age Events and Worship

ADVENT

CHRISTMAS

EPIPHANY

LENT

I HAVE CALLED
YOU — YOU
ARE
MINE

HERE I AM, LORD

A PURE HEART
CREATE FOR ME

EASTER

EASTER

PENTECOST

TRINITY

ALL SAINTS

HARVEST

GENERAL

GENERAL